THE U.S. DEPARTMENT OF THE TREASURY'S ANALYSIS OF THE SITUATION IN PUERTO RICO

OVERSIGHT HEARING

BEFORE THE

COMMITTEE ON NATURAL RESOURCES U.S. HOUSE OF REPRESENTATIVES

ONE HUNDRED FOURTEENTH CONGRESS

SECOND SESSION

Thursday, February 25, 2016

Serial No. 114–34

Printed for the use of the Committee on Natural Resources

Available via the World Wide Web: http://www.fdsys.gov
or
Committee address: http://naturalresources.house.gov

U.S. GOVERNMENT PUBLISHING OFFICE

98–879 PDF   WASHINGTON : 2016

For sale by the Superintendent of Documents, U.S. Government Publishing Office
Internet: bookstore.gpo.gov   Phone: toll free (866) 512–1800; DC area (202) 512–1800
Fax: (202) 512–2104   Mail: Stop IDCC, Washington, DC 20402–0001

COMMITTEE ON NATURAL RESOURCES

ROB BISHOP, UT, *Chairman*
RAÚL M. GRIJALVA, AZ, *Ranking Democratic Member*

Don Young, AK
Louie Gohmert, TX
Doug Lamborn, CO
Robert J. Wittman, VA
John Fleming, LA
Tom McClintock, CA
Glenn Thompson, PA
Cynthia M. Lummis, WY
Dan Benishek, MI
Jeff Duncan, SC
Paul A. Gosar, AZ
Raúl R. Labrador, ID
Doug LaMalfa, CA
Jeff Denham, CA
Paul Cook, CA
Bruce Westerman, AR
Garret Graves, LA
Dan Newhouse, WA
Ryan K. Zinke, MT
Jody B. Hice, GA
Aumua Amata Coleman Radewagen, AS
Thomas MacArthur, NJ
Alexander X. Mooney, WV
Cresent Hardy, NV
Darin LaHood, IL

Grace F. Napolitano, CA
Madeleine Z. Bordallo, GU
Jim Costa, CA
Gregorio Kilili Camacho Sablan, CNMI
Niki Tsongas, MA
Pedro R. Pierluisi, PR
Jared Huffman, CA
Raul Ruiz, CA
Alan S. Lowenthal, CA
Matt Cartwright, PA
Donald S. Beyer, Jr., VA
Norma J. Torres, CA
Debbie Dingell, MI
Ruben Gallego, AZ
Lois Capps, CA
Jared Polis, CO
Wm. Lacy Clay, MO

Jason Knox, *Chief of Staff*
Lisa Pittman, *Chief Counsel*
David Watkins, *Democratic Staff Director*
Sarah Lim, *Democratic Chief Counsel*

———

(II)

CONTENTS

OVERSIGHT HEARING ON THE U.S. DEPARTMENT OF THE TREASURY'S ANALYSIS OF THE SITUATION IN PUERTO RICO

Thursday, February 25, 2016
U.S. House of Representatives
Committee on Natural Resources
Washington, DC

The committee met, pursuant to notice, at 10:09 a.m., in room 1324, Longworth House Office Building, Hon. Rob Bishop [Chairman of the Committee] presiding.

Present: Representatives Bishop, Gohmert, Lamborn, McClintock, Thompson, Lummis, Duncan, Labrador, LaMalfa, Westerman, Graves, Zinke, Hice, MacArthur, Hardy, LaHood; Grijalva, Bordallo, Tsongas, Pierluisi, Huffman, Beyer, Torres, Dingell, Gallego, Polis, and Clay.

Also present: Representatives Serrano, Gutierrez, and Velazquez.

The CHAIRMAN. All right, we will call this committee hearing to order. We appreciate those who are here today, both Members and the witnesses.

STATEMENT OF THE HON. ROB BISHOP, A REPRESENTATIVE IN CONGRESS FROM THE STATE OF UTAH

The CHAIRMAN. This oversight hearing is the third we have had in a couple of months, and it is going to focus on the Administration's perspective on the Puerto Rico situation. I appreciate Mr. Weiss being here. He is the sole witness that we will have this morning.

If you recall the first hearing that we had, we focused on the opportunity for private investment, the importance of modernizing Puerto Rico's energy infrastructure, and we touched on the potential for voluntary debt restructuring agreements that could be reached by both creditors and debtors.

In our second hearing, we discussed the merits of establishing some kind of an oversight body that will ensure economic stability and revitalization in Puerto Rico. And I think that is also one of the key elements, we have to have the revitalization there, too. I think this committee is uniquely situated to provide those kinds of recommendations that can actually help grow the economy. We are not just going to try and settle things out; we have to grow the economy, or at least give the potential for growth in the economy that has to be there.

There is some common ground. There are some shared ideas of a need for strong fiscal governance and also transparency. But we also have some shared ideas of debt restructuring, and we must facilitate good faith negotiations between creditors and debtors at all times. There have to be those kinds of appropriate encouragements for all parties to reach consensual agreements.

So, both the Administration and the committee seek to have a productive outcome for Puerto Rico and its citizens and there are still some open questions of how we will do that. I trust that Mr. Weiss will be able to shed more light on the areas of potential agreement between the Administration and this particular committee, and I look forward to continuing the dialogue as we reach some specific solutions that will be introduced shortly.

[The prepared statement of Mr. Bishop follows:]

PREPARED STATEMENT OF THE HON. ROB BISHOP, CHAIRMAN, COMMITTEE ON NATURAL RESOURCES

Let me begin by reiterating this committee's purpose and intent concerning Puerto Rico. The bill this committee produces will be to secure Puerto Rico's future for its 3.5 million American citizens, respect their authority to self-govern, restore credibility to the Puerto Rican economy, and instill principles of good governance and fiscal transparency to encourage private investment and promote sustainability.

Today's oversight hearing—the third in 2 months—focuses on the Administration's perspective on the Puerto Rico situation.

During the first hearing, the committee addressed the opportunity for private investment to modernize Puerto Rico's outdated energy infrastructure, and touched on the potential for voluntary debt restructuring agreements to be reached between creditors and debtors. At the second hearing, we discussed the merit of establishing an independent oversight body to ensure that Puerto Rico is on the path toward economic stability and revitalization.

In some way, the conclusions reached in the first two hearings touch on or parallel the Administration's proposals for relieving the fiscal crisis in Puerto Rico.

There is common ground. First, there is the shared idea of a need for strong fiscal governance and oversight that provides "sufficient safeguards to ensure Puerto Rico adheres to its recovery plan and fully implements proposed reforms." [1]

Such oversight is the starting point for any legislative proposal that will be forthcoming from this committee. We must provide the Puerto Rican economy and people a path forward—and that may only be accomplished if an independent oversight body has the strength and ability to encourage the reinvigoration of the island's economic prospects.

The Administration's proposal seeks to respect the "autonomy" of Puerto Rico. I hope today's discussion will provide clarity as to what the Administration means by that term—specifically, how deferential any oversight authority must be to the Puerto Rican government, and how such deference is reconcilable with necessity for reform, given the track record of the Commonwealth's government.

Another pillar supporting the Administration's platform is a call for Puerto Rico to have access to debt restructuring. Let me be clear on this topic, Puerto Rico already has the tools to restructure through voluntary negotiations a large portion— if not all—of its debt. Indeed, the restructuring of PREPA exemplifies the type of deal that should be encouraged for as much Puerto Rican debt as possible. Therefore, we must do all we can to facilitate the development of consensual agreements between all creditors and debtors—and to ensure that such negotiations occur in good faith.

Last—today's witness, Mr. Weiss through testimony before a recent Senate hearing identified the need for measures to boost economic growth and ensure a level playing field in Federal healthcare benefits. Unfortunately, all of the Administration's proposals concerning the Earned Income Tax Credit and Medicaid fall far outside the jurisdictional bounds of this committee. That said, we are interested in the Administration's position on what can be done to encourage private investment to come into Puerto Rico.

It is clear, both the Administration and this committee seek a positive outcome for Puerto Rico and its citizens. How we get there is still an open question. I trust that Mr. Weiss will be able to shed more light on areas of potential agreement between the Administration and this committee, and I look forward to the dialogue toward real solutions.

---

[1] This quote is taken from the White House's published plan on Puerto Rico, entitled: "Addressing Puerto Rico's Economic and Fiscal Crisis and Creating a Path to Recovery: Roadmap for Congressional Action."

The CHAIRMAN. With that, I am going to yield to Mr. Grijalva for his opening statement.

STATEMENT OF THE HON. RAÚL M. GRIJALVA, A REPRESENTATIVE IN CONGRESS FROM THE STATE OF ARIZONA

Mr. GRIJALVA. Thank you, Mr. Chairman. I will enter my full statement into the record, if there is no objection.

The CHAIRMAN. Can I stop you if there is an objection?

Mr. GRIJALVA. If you want to hear it, I would be more than glad to——

The CHAIRMAN. No objection.

[The prepared statement of Mr. Grijalva follows:]

PREPARED STATEMENT OF THE HON. RAÚL M. GRIJALVA, RANKING MEMBER, COMMITTEE ON NATURAL RESOURCES

Thank you. Mr. Chairman, I want to begin by welcoming our witness today and to commend him for the assistance he has been providing to leaders of Puerto Rico to deal with the crisis they are facing.

Today's hearing, Mr. Chairman, will be the third we have held in this committee since Congress reconvened in January and since Speaker Ryan instructed relevant committees to report out legislation on Puerto Rico by the end of March.

While these hearings are instructive, if we are going to meet the Speaker's deadline, we should have long since begun discussions on a bipartisan legislative solution to the crisis. In fact, the Ranking Member of the Judiciary Committee and I issued the same call in a letter we sent 4 weeks ago to you, Mr. Chairman, as well as to the Chairman of the Judiciary Committee. As of today, we are still awaiting your invitation to begin those discussions. Maybe the invitation was lost in the mail.

In the meantime, while we fiddle by holding yet another hearing, Rome—which in this case is Puerto Rico—continues to burn.

As I have mentioned before, Puerto Rico is currently insolvent and has lost access to the credit markets even at very high interest rates. Last June, Governor Garcia Padilla announced that Puerto Rico could not pay its debts after which his government defaulted on bond payments in August and again this January.

Since then, the government has withheld paying tax refunds and payments to healthcare agencies causing several hospitals to close. Additionally, businesses are leaving the island causing the government to collect even less revenue than expected.

This is all occurring in the face of the fact that the Puerto Rican people have already endured more than a decade of austerity. Over the last few years, the government of Puerto Rico has hiked the sales tax to the highest in the United States, raised tuition at public universities, increased the cost of water and electricity, twice upped the tax on gasoline, and raised the retirement age. Puerto Rico now has a 45 percent poverty rate because of these measures.

In the meantime, the island continues to bleed residents, who see relocation to Florida or elsewhere on the mainland as their only hope for survival. By some estimates, up to 100,000 Puerto Ricans left the island last year.

I want to again commend you, Mr. Weiss, Secretary Lew, and President Obama for the comprehensive proposal you put forth last year for a legislative solution to the Puerto Rican crisis.

From what we are hearing, there appears to be agreement on the general outline for a legislative fix for Puerto Rico: an oversight board and broad restructuring authority. If this is indeed the case, there is nothing preventing us, once this hearing is concluded, from immediately drafting bipartisan legislation that can be reported to the Floor without further delay.

As we begin our deliberations, we must ask ourselves who wins and who loses in each scenario. As for who wins when we blindly demand more budget cuts, a report released by my staff last summer answers that question. So-called austerity is a tool used by hedge funds to boost their profits at the expense of the men, women and children of Puerto Rico. A control board that would use austerity to help hedge funds lock in those profits, no matter the human cost, is not the answer. We can and we must do better than that.

The CHAIRMAN. I now recognize Mrs. Lummis for an opening statement from the Vice Chair.

STATEMENT OF THE HON. CYNTHIA M. LUMMIS, A REPRESENTATIVE IN CONGRESS FROM THE STATE OF WYOMING

Mrs. LUMMIS. Thank you, Mr. Chairman, and thank you for setting up the tone of this committee today. We have with us Mr. Antonio Weiss, Counselor of the Secretary of the Treasury. He will share with us the U.S. Department of the Treasury's analysis of the situation in Puerto Rico.

We hope, Mr. Weiss, that you can help the committee as we continue to work toward legislation to advance good governance, as well as fiscal transparency and accountability. I hope you will also have some ideas about how we can improve the economy of those living in Puerto Rico. We welcome continuing that discussion, even some of those ideas that are not specifically within the jurisdiction of the Natural Resources Committee.

We very much appreciate your being with us here today. We look forward to hearing from you and the other Members as we try to bring some clarity toward this issue, and bring a solution about that is good for the people of Puerto Rico and the United States.

Thank you, Mr. Chairman, I yield back.

[The prepared statement of Mrs. Lummis follows:]

PREPARED STATEMENT OF THE HON. CYNTHIA M. LUMMIS, A REPRESENTATIVE IN CONGRESS FROM THE STATE OF WYOMING

Thank you all for joining me for this hearing of the Natural Resources Committee to examine the ongoing economic crisis in Puerto Rico. This is the latest in a series of hearings by the Natural Resources Committee regarding Puerto Rico. Today we have with us Mr. Antonio F. Weiss, Counselor to the Secretary of the Treasury. He will share with us the U.S. Department of the Treasury's analysis of the situation in Puerto Rico.

I hope he can help the committee as we look to work on legislation to advance good governance as well as fiscal transparency and accountability. I am sure he will also have some ideas about how we can spur economic growth and improve the economy of those living in Puerto Rico. We obviously welcome continuing that discussion, but many of the proposals we have heard previously are not within the jurisdiction of the Natural Resources Committee.

Mr. Weiss, I appreciate you being here with us today. I look forward to hearing from you and the other Members as we try to bring some clarity to what is going on here and build toward a solution.

———

The CHAIRMAN. Thank you.

And I think, Mr. Pierluisi, you are probably going to be one of the key players in this issue, I am assuming. We will recognize you for an opening statement, as well.

STATEMENT OF THE HON. PEDRO R. PIERLUISI, A DELEGATE FROM THE TERRITORY OF PUERTO RICO

Mr. PIERLUISI. Thank you, Chairman. At a Senate hearing last year, the Governor of Puerto Rico compared the territory to a ship at sea issuing a distress call to Congress. I want to clarify this metaphor. The passengers on this ship are not only the 3.5 million U.S. citizens that reside in Puerto Rico. They are also individuals and institutions located in Puerto Rico and the states that own bonds issued by the territory and its instrumentalities.

Puerto Rico and its creditors are on the same ship. We are going to sail safely to shore together or we are going to sink together. Our common fate depends on whether leaders in Washington and San Juan rise to the occasion. Principled compromise is the only course to harbor.

How did our ship arrive in such perilous waters in the first place? Precisely, because over the years the people of Puerto Rico have been poorly served by their national and local leaders. In Puerto Rico, inequality at the national level has led to mismanagement at the local level. Federal policy toward Puerto Rico is a national disgrace, contradicting the claim that the United States desires democracy and dignity for all of its citizens.

Under this policy, my constituents are American enough to fight for this country, a duty they have performed proudly since World War I. But they are not American enough to vote for President, Senators, or voting Members of the House. They are American enough to win nine Medals of Honor and to form the backbone of a U.S. Army unit that recently earned the Congressional Gold Medal, but they are not American enough to receive fair treatment under Federal programs that improve quality of life and promote work.

And so, they are moving to the states in huge numbers because it is human nature to go where you have the best chance to survive and thrive. The excuse given by Federal policymakers for such disparate treatment is always the same: "You don't pay Federal taxes," they proclaim. Never mind that individuals and businesses in Puerto Rico pay about $3.6 billion in Federal taxes to the IRS every year. Never mind that it was Congress, not Puerto Rico, that chose to exempt island residents from certain Federal income taxes. And never mind that, because the Federal tax code combines tax obligations with tax credits, the average working family in Puerto Rico contributes more in Federal payroll and income taxes than the average working family in the states.

As a statehood supporter, I aspire for American citizens in Puerto Rico to have the same rights and responsibilities as American citizens in every state. I do not appreciate being told the appalling treatment we receive as a territory is, in fact, preferential treatment.

To compensate for the shortfall in Federal support, political leaders in Puerto Rico have tended to overtax local residents and businesses, impeding economic growth, and to over-borrow in the bond market, creating excessive deficits and debts. Under certain administrations in San Juan, policymaking crossed the line from imprudent to negligent. We, in Puerto Rico, must accept this fact, resolve to do better in the future, and refuse to repeat the mistakes of the past.

If our ship is to weather this storm, Congress must enact legislation that authorizes Puerto Rico to restructure a meaningful portion of its debt in a fair and orderly manner, which will ultimately benefit Puerto Rico and the vast majority of its creditors.

Today, we will have a constructive conversation about the contours of this debt restructuring mechanism, but it is no longer reasonable to question whether such a mechanism is needed at all.

In addition, because inequality has bred mismanagement, the bill should address both cause and effect. The bill cannot fix every disparity Puerto Rico faces, because only statehood can do that. But it should make a good faith effort to rectify certain disparities, and it is important to emphasize that Puerto Rico and its creditors agree on this point.

Finally, I understand that the issue of an independent oversight board is a sensitive one, especially for a territory that has no democracy at the national level. However, if the composition and powers of the board are properly calibrated, the board will supplement, not displace, local elected officials. If Puerto Rico officials act in a disciplined way, the board will be dissolved within a short period of time. It is my sense that the people of Puerto Rico recognize the potential benefits of an independent board; and it is the people, not island politicians, that matter most.

Mr. Chairman, following this hearing it is my hope and expectation that we will craft a balanced and bipartisan bill that can be enacted into law. Thank you.

[The prepared statement of Mr. Pierluisi follows:]

PREPARED STATEMENT OF THE HON. PEDRO R. PIERLUISI, A DELEGATE FROM THE TERRITORY OF PUERTO RICO

Thank you, Chairman Bishop. At a Senate hearing last year, the Governor of Puerto Rico compared the territory to a ship at sea, issuing a distress call to Congress. I want to clarify this metaphor. The passengers on this ship are not only the 3.5 million U.S. citizens that reside in Puerto Rico. They are also the individuals and institutions, located in Puerto Rico and the states, that own bonds issued by the territory and its instrumentalities.

Puerto Rico and its creditors are on the same ship. We are going to sail safely to shore together, or we are going to sink together. Our common fate depends on whether leaders in Washington and San Juan rise to the occasion.

Principled compromise is the only course to harbor. How did our ship arrive in such perilous waters in the first place? Precisely because, over the years, the people of Puerto Rico have been poorly served by their national and local leaders.

In Puerto Rico, inequality at the national level has led to mismanagement at the local level. Federal policy toward Puerto Rico is a national disgrace, contradicting the claim that the United States desires democracy and dignity for all of its citizens. Under this policy, my constituents are American enough to serve, fight and die for this country—a duty they have performed proudly since World War I. But they are not American enough to vote for President, Senators or voting Members of the House. They are American enough to win nine Medals of Honor, and to form the backbone of a U.S. Army unit that recently earned the Congressional Gold Medal. But, as long as they remain in Puerto Rico, my constituents are not American enough to receive fair treatment under Federal programs that improve quality of life and promote work. And so they are moving to the states in huge numbers, because it is human nature to go where you have the best chance to survive and to thrive.

The excuse given by Federal policymakers for such disparate treatment is always the same. "You don't pay Federal taxes," they proclaim. Never mind that individuals and businesses in Puerto Rico pay about $3.6 billion in Federal taxes to the IRS every year. Never mind that it was Congress, not Puerto Rico, that chose to exempt island residents from certain Federal income taxes. And never mind that because the Federal tax code combines tax obligations with tax credits, the average working family in Puerto Rico contributes more in Federal payroll and income taxes than the average working family in the states. As a statehood supporter, I aspire for American citizens in Puerto Rico to have the same rights and responsibilities as American citizens in every state. I don't appreciate being told—falsely—that the appalling treatment we receive as a territory is, in fact, preferential treatment.

As noted, inequality at the national level has enabled, even compelled, mismanagement at the local level. To compensate for the shortfall in Federal support, political leaders in Puerto Rico have tended to over-tax local residents and businesses, impeding economic growth, and to over-borrow in the bond market, creating excessive deficits and debt. Under certain administrations in San Juan, policy-making crossed the line from imprudent to negligent. We in Puerto Rico must be candid and courageous, accepting rather than denying this fact, resolving to do better in the future and refusing to repeat the mistakes of the past. Discipline is required, and so disciplined we must be.

If our ship is to weather the present storm, Congress must enact legislation that authorizes Puerto Rico to restructure a meaningful portion of its debt in a fair and orderly manner, a step that will ultimately benefit Puerto Rico and the vast majority of its creditors. Today we will have a constructive conversation about the contours of this debt restructuring mechanism, but it is no longer reasonable to question whether such a mechanism is needed at all.

In addition, because inequality has bred mismanagement, the bill should address both cause and effect. With respect to the former, the bill cannot fix every disparity Puerto Rico faces, because only statehood can do that, but it should make a good-faith effort to rectify certain disparities—and it is important to emphasize that Puerto Rico and its creditors agree on the point.

With respect to the latter, I understand that the issue of an independent oversight board is a sensitive one, especially for a territory that has no democracy at the national level. Three points are in order.

First, if the composition and powers of the board are properly calibrated, the board will supplement—not displace—local elected officials. Second, if Puerto Rico officials act in a disciplined way, the board will be dissolved within a short period of time. Finally, it is my sense that the people of Puerto Rico recognize the potential benefits of a temporary board, and it is the people—not island politicians—that matter most.

Following this hearing, it is my hope and expectation that Congress will craft a balanced and bipartisan bill that can be enacted into law.

Thank you.

———

The CHAIRMAN. Thank you very much. I appreciate that. I am going to ask unanimous consent that all other Members' opening statements, if they have any, are made part of the hearing record if they are submitted to the Clerk by 5:00 p.m. today. I am also going to ask unanimous consent that my full statement be added into the record, instead of giving it right now.

[No response.]

The CHAIRMAN. Without objection, so ordered.

I am also asking unanimous consent as we start, that the gentleman from New York, Mr. Serrano; the gentlewoman from New York, Ms. Velazquez; and the gentleman from Illinois, Mr. Gutierrez, be allowed to sit on the dais and participate in today's hearing.

[No response.]

The CHAIRMAN. If no objections, so ordered.

With that, we are honored to have Mr. Weiss here with us.

We are going to turn to you for your opening statement, and then we will get to the questions that are before us.

Hopefully, you know how the clock works. It is a 5-minute opening statement, but I think you are the only witness, so we can be a little bit flexible if we need to.

Mr. WEISS. Thank you for that.

STATEMENT OF ANTONIO WEISS, COUNSELOR TO THE SECRETARY, U.S. DEPARTMENT OF THE TREASURY, WASHINGTON, DC

Mr. WEISS. Chairman Bishop, Ranking Member Grijalva, and members of the committee, thank you for inviting Treasury to testify today. We commend this committee and its staff for its leadership in response to the March timetable for action set by Speaker Ryan. We look forward to working together on a responsible solution to this crisis. There is a growing recognition that we need to act now. We are encouraged by the positive, bipartisan discussions that are taking place.

This is a Puerto Rican crisis, which means it is an American crisis. Puerto Rico is home to 3.5 million Americans whose economic well-being and safety are at stake. In the many months that we have been traveling to Puerto Rico and meeting with government officials, business leaders, and workers, there is a growing sense of fear and a more urgent call to action.

Puerto Rico is already in distress. What started as a recession has turned into a fiscal and liquidity crisis that shows signs of becoming a humanitarian one, as well. Health, education, and public safety services have been curtailed because the government simply cannot pay all of its bills.

The government remains open only because the Governor has authorized more than $1 billion in onerous and unsustainable emergency liquidity actions. Tax refunds have been withheld from citizens. Pension assets, already severely depleted, are being sold to fund central government operations. Money dedicated to one group of creditors is being taken to pay other creditors. The inevitable defaults and litigation have already begun.

Without action, this crisis can only escalate. The Government Development Bank, which is at the heart of the financial system, is dangerously under-capitalized. Debt payments in May and July, including more than $800 million of constitutionally prioritized debt, are unlikely to be made. Mounting litigation will flood the courts and the central government itself could be forced to shut down entirely.

There is no room for error in this economy. Fifty-seven percent of children live in poverty. Unemployment is 12.2 percent, which is more than twice the national average. The population has dropped by 10 percent in the past decade, including 2.5 percent last year alone, as young, working-age Puerto Ricans leave the island with their children in search of opportunity. Their departure leaves behind an aging population and further erodes Puerto Rico's long-term growth prospects.

Under any realistic scenario, Puerto Rico's $70 billion of debt is not sustainable and markets know this. Puerto Rico bonds trade between 10 and 70 cents on the dollar. The debt is enormously complex, with 18 different issuers and 20 creditor committees already with competing claims. As the cascading defaults and litigation unfold, there is real risk of another lost decade, this one more dangerous than the last.

What is the solution? In October of last year, the Administration released a comprehensive plan to stem the crisis and to restore economic growth. While we believe that all elements of our plan are essential, I would like to focus today on the most time-sensitive components: debt restructuring and fiscal oversight.

First, restructuring. We propose a restructuring authority pursuant to the territorial clause of the U.S. Constitution, that would apply to all of the Commonwealth's liabilities. Importantly, this authority would expressly not apply to states, who have an entirely different relationship with the Federal Government under the 10th Amendment.

In our view, all creditors must be at the table to reach a comprehensive and sustainable solution. But we are not advocating a one-size-fits-all approach. Restructuring legislation can be designed to consider existing priorities and claims. We would also favor allowing for an initial period of voluntary negotiations with creditors, facilitated by a stay on litigation.

Second, oversight. We propose strong, independent Federal oversight to address the Commonwealth's long history of fiscal mismanagement and inadequate financial disclosure. Access to a restructuring authority should be strictly conditioned on acceptance of this oversight. But to be effective, oversight should be structured in a way that respects Puerto Rico's self-governance, while assuring implementation of required reforms.

We believe Federal legislation can be crafted to achieve that balance.

Pairing restructuring and oversight is a tried and true combination to resolve debt crises, both domestically and abroad. However, these two proposals must be enacted together. One without the other will not work, and these two provisions would cost U.S. taxpayers nothing.

Municipal bond investors tell us that an orderly restructuring under clear Federal guidelines is also the surest way to restore Puerto Rico's market access, and it is the best outcome for municipal markets, far preferable to a protracted, disorderly series of defaults of unprecedented magnitude and complexity. The question is not whether the Commonwealth will emerge from this crisis, but when, and at what cost to the 3.5 million Americans on the island.

In closing, we look forward to working with this committee on legislation that will protect our fellow citizens in Puerto Rico.

[The prepared statement of Mr. Weiss follows:]

PREPARED STATEMENT OF MR. ANTONIO WEISS, COUNSELOR TO THE SECRETARY, U.S. DEPARTMENT OF THE TREASURY

Chairman Bishop, Ranking Member Grijalva, and members of the committee, thank you for inviting Treasury to testify today. We commend this committee for its leadership in response to the March timetable for action set by Speaker Ryan. We look forward to working together on a responsible solution to this crisis. There is a growing recognition that we need to act now, and we are encouraged by the positive, bipartisan discussions taking place.

This is a Puerto Rican crisis, which means it is an American crisis.

Puerto Rico is home to 3.5 million Americans whose economic well-being and safety are at stake. In the many months we have been traveling to Puerto Rico and meeting with government officials, business leaders and workers, there is a growing sense of fear and a more urgent call to action.

ACTION IS NEEDED NOW

Puerto Rico is already in distress. What started as a recession has turned into a fiscal and liquidity crisis that shows signs of becoming a humanitarian one as well.

The Commonwealth has begun defaulting on its debt. Puerto Rico no longer has access to the credit markets, even the costliest ones. Health, education, and public safety services have been curtailed because the government cannot pay all of its bills. Hospitals are closing doors and businesses are leaving the Island.

The government remains open only because the Governor authorized more than $1 billion in onerous and unsustainable emergency liquidity actions. Tax refunds have been withheld from citizens. Pension assets, already severely depleted, are being sold to fund government operations. Money dedicated to one group of creditors is being taken to pay other creditors. The inevitable defaults and lawsuits have already begun.

Without action, this crisis will escalate. The Government Development Bank, which is at the heart of Puerto Rico's financial system, is dangerously undercapitalized. Debt payments in May and July, including nearly $800 million of constitutionally prioritized debt, are unlikely to be made. Mounting litigation will flood the courts. And the central government itself could be forced to shut down entirely.

There is no room for error in this economy. 57 percent of children live in poverty. Unemployment is 12.2 percent, more than twice the national average. At $19,000, median annual household income in Puerto Rico is approximately one-third the U.S. median.

This crisis has sparked the largest wave of out-migration from Puerto Rico since the 1950s. The population has dropped by nearly 10 percent in the past decade—and 2.5 percent last year alone—as young, working age Puerto Ricans leave the Island with their children in search of opportunity. Since World War II, no U.S. state has posted such a large 10-year drop in population.

Puerto Ricans are leaving from across the socioeconomic spectrum. Their departure leaves behind an aging population and further erodes Puerto Rico's long-term growth prospects. Seniors already represent more than 23 percent of the population, one of the highest ratios in the country, and the number of children under 5 years of age has decreased 37 percent since 2000.[1] Only an end to the crisis and a return to growth can stop this vicious cycle.

THE DEBT IS NOT SUSTAINABLE

Under any realistic scenario, Puerto Rico's $70 billion of debt is not sustainable. Markets know this. Puerto Rico bonds trade between 10 and 70 cents on the dollar. Debt service consumes one-third of all central government revenues, more than five times the average state. A balanced budget would require a primary surplus of 5 percent of Gross National Product (GNP), significantly above the level that any distressed entity can reasonably sustain.

In addition, the Commonwealth has a $46 billion pension liability funded by only $2 billion in net assets, the lowest level of any major pension system in the country. More than 330,000 current and future beneficiaries rely on the public pension system as their primary source of retirement security. Average payments in the largest system are less than $1,200 per month. A failure to protect those payments would irreparably harm retirees and add greater stress to Puerto Rico's economy.

A COMPREHENSIVE RESPONSE IS NEEDED

The depth and complexity of Puerto Rico's financial challenges led the Administration to release a comprehensive legislative roadmap last October to stem the crisis and restore growth. The plan includes a debt restructuring authority paired with fiscal oversight, healthcare transformation, and tax incentives to reward work.[2] Our proposals have drawn strong support from business, religious and labor leaders as well as conservative economists and the *Wall Street Journal*.

While we believe all elements of our plan are essential to Puerto Rico's recovery and long-term growth, the most time-sensitive components are debt restructuring and fiscal oversight.

PUERTO RICO NEEDS TOOLS TO RESTRUCTURE ALL OF ITS FINANCIAL LIABILITIES

Puerto Rico has already defaulted on its debt and is facing a likely series of future defaults of unprecedented magnitude in the municipal bond market. The debt is unusually complex with 18 different issuers and 20 creditor committees with competing claims. There is currently no way to forestall litigation or conclude a voluntary agreement supported by a majority of creditors.

We propose a restructuring authority, pursuant to the territorial clause of the U.S. Constitution, that would apply to all of the Commonwealth's liabilities. This would give Puerto Rico the tools it needs to reach a resolution with creditors and adjust its debts to a sustainable level. Importantly, this authority would expressly not apply to states, who have an entirely different relationship with the Federal

---

[1] Puerto Rico Fiscal and Economic Growth Plan, released September 9, 2015. Page 9. Available at: http://www.gdb-pur.com/documents/PuertoRicoFiscalandEconomicGrowthPlan9.9.15.pdf.
[2] "Addressing Puerto Rico's Economic and Fiscal Crisis and Creating a Path to Recovery: Roadmap for Congressional Action." Dated October 21, 2015. Available at: https://www.whitehouse.gov/sites/default/files/roadmap_for_congressional_action_puerto_rico_final.pdf.

Government under the 10th Amendment. Accessing this territorial restructuring authority would be conditioned on acceptance of strong, independent Federal oversight.

A territorial restructuring framework would consist of: (1) a temporary stay on litigation to protect the provision of vital public services and allow time for voluntary negotiations; (2) a voting mechanism to prevent a few hold-outs from blocking a reasonable compromise; and (3) if negotiations fail, a court-supervised structure to assure an orderly resolution.

Without a comprehensive restructuring framework, Puerto Rico will continue to default on its debt, and litigation will intensify. It will be contentious and protracted—both among competing creditor classes and against the Commonwealth—while the economy worsens and Puerto Rico's capacity to repay creditors collapses further. As the cascading defaults and litigation unfold, there is real risk of another lost decade, this one more damaging than the last.

In our view, all creditors must be at the table to reach a comprehensive and sustainable solution. But we are not advocating a "one size fits all" approach; restructuring legislation can be designed to consider existing priorities and claims. We would also favor allowing for an initial period of voluntary negotiations with creditors, facilitated by a stay on litigation.

Any viable solution will require restructuring Puerto Rico's liabilities to a level its economy can safely and reasonably afford.

EFFECTIVE OVERSIGHT IS ALSO REQUIRED TO STRENGTHEN PUERTO RICO'S FISCAL GOVERNANCE

We propose strong, independent Federal oversight to address the Commonwealth's longstanding history of fiscal mismanagement and inadequate financial disclosure. Accounting and payroll systems are antiquated and insufficiently integrated. Disclosure remains opaque and financial reporting deadlines are repeatedly missed.

Strong, independent oversight is needed. But, to be effective, oversight should be structured in a way that respects Puerto Rico's self-governance while assuring implementation of required reforms.

We believe Federal legislation can be crafted to achieve this balance.

Pairing restructuring and oversight is a tried and true combination to resolve debt crises, both domestically and abroad. However, these two proposals must be enacted together. One without the other will not work. Oversight and restructuring, appropriately adapted to Puerto Rico, would put the Commonwealth on a path to fiscal recovery and renewed economic growth.

Importantly, these two provisions would cost U.S. taxpayers nothing.

CONGRESS MUST ALSO FIX PUERTO RICO'S HEALTHCARE INADEQUACIES AND REWARD WORK

The Medicaid programs in Puerto Rico and the other the U.S. territories are fundamentally different from the Medicaid program in the states. Medicaid funding in the territories is capped; beneficiaries are offered fewer benefits; and the Federal Government contributes less on a per-capita basis than it does to the rest of the Nation.

The Commonwealth provides health insurance coverage to approximately 1.5 million Medicaid beneficiaries, representing nearly half of Puerto Rico's total population.

When one-time Affordable Care Act funds are exhausted in Puerto Rico, as early as June 2017, up to 600,000 Americans living in Puerto Rico could lose their healthcare coverage. To avoid this calamity, Congress needs to reform Puerto Rico's Medicaid program to raise the standard of care and prevent Medicaid's unstable financing from exacerbating Puerto Rico's fiscal crisis.

These constraints on Puerto Rico's Medicaid program also limit Puerto Rico's capacity to respond to emergent healthcare threats like the Zika virus. That is why the Department of Health and Human Services recently requested a supplemental appropriation from Congress to enact a temporary 1-year increase in the territories' Federal Medicaid share.

In addition to fixing Puerto Rico's inadequate healthcare treatment, Congress must also enact some of the most proven, bipartisan tools for stimulating economic growth and rewarding work. A large body of economic research, including Treasury's own analysis, has found the Earned Income Tax Credit (EITC) is one of the strongest, most powerful policy tools to meet those objectives. As a result, Congress should grant Puerto Rico access to an EITC.

I would now like to respond to four thoughtful questions Chairman Bishop and his staff have raised as they work to design a responsible legislative solution.

For those who support authorizing restructuring authority for Puerto Rico, will the Commonwealth ever be able to access the markets again?

Yes. An orderly restructuring framework paired with effective oversight would help remove legal uncertainties, improve fiscal governance and return Puerto Rico to the kind of economic growth that attracts market capital.

Numerous U.S. cities have regained market access after fiscal restructuring and oversight, including New York City, Washington, DC, Cleveland and Philadelphia. Notable companies such as General Motors, Delta, and Texaco, have also undergone restructuring and emerged stronger and better than before. Debt investors understand restructuring can lead to better outcomes for all parties. Puerto Rico should expect to achieve the same result.

Puerto Rico has not had access to the municipal market for more than 2 years. Municipal bond investors tell us that an orderly restructuring under clear Federal guidelines is also the surest way to restore Puerto Rico's market access. And, it is the best outcome for municipal markets—far preferable to a protracted, disorderly series of defaults of unprecedented magnitude and complexity. A post-restructured Puerto Rico that can pay its debts, invest in infrastructure and support economic growth should attract traditional investors to consider new investment.

For those who oppose authorizing restructuring authority, will recalcitrant creditor holdouts ever seriously negotiate without restructuring authority?

No. Without access to territorial restructuring authority that brings all creditors to the table, it is overwhelmingly likely that holdouts will prevent voluntary negotiations from reaching a successful conclusion.

In addition, proposals that only provide access to Chapter 9 of the Bankruptcy Code will not resolve this crisis. Less than one-third of Puerto Rico's debt would be clearly eligible for adjustment under Chapter 9. The remaining debt is either ineligible or, like many other recent Chapter 9 cases, would likely go through protracted litigation regarding eligibility for restructuring. The litigation could take many years to resolve, pushing the Commonwealth further into a downward economic spiral. Additionally, because Chapter 9 is limited to certain public corporations and municipalities, it leaves Puerto Rico's central government liabilities, including general obligation bonds and employee pensions, outside the reach of restructuring.

Chapter 9 was carefully designed for states, in conformance with the 10th Amendment of the U.S. Constitution, to enable municipalities to adjust their liabilities. Puerto Rico is neither a state nor a municipality. What we need here is a tailored solution permitted under the U.S. Constitution to address the complex, interconnected liability structure of an entire territory.

For those who support establishing just a Federal advisory board without fiscal enforcement powers, will Puerto Rico ever make the necessary reforms to improve their fiscal governance?

An advisory board is not adequate to do the job. But, there are various ways to create a strong, independent oversight board while simultaneously preserving Puerto Rico's self-governance.

First, Puerto Rico's access to restructuring authorities, including an automatic stay on litigation, should be strictly conditioned on the Commonwealth's acceptance of Federal oversight.

Second, the board should provide independent revenue forecasts and recommend improvements to budgetary and fiscal management practices. This includes regular, multi-year fiscal plans and budgets that are balanced pursuant to generally accepted accounting principles. The board should also have adequate enforcement tools to ensure necessary adjustments are made if the government falls short of its targets.

Third, while the oversight board should not be responsible for direct negotiations with creditors, it should support the Commonwealth's restructuring efforts. For example, the board should certify that any voluntary restructuring agreements between the Commonwealth and its creditors meet certain criteria. In addition, authorization from the board should be required before Puerto Rico gets access to territorial restructuring authorities.

Fourth, the oversight board should be based in San Juan and have a majority representation of Puerto Ricans, but retain the independence that would result from appointments pursuant to Federal law. Members must have relevant expertise and no conflicts of interest. The board should be granted flexibility to hire professional staff with the skills and experience to make this effort successful.

Last, an oversight board should remain in place until the necessary fiscal reforms are carried out, budgets are balanced, and market access returns.

For those who prefer a dominant Federal control board, how will you get the needed buy-in to make lasting reforms that will ensure Puerto Rico does not find itself in this position again?

Respecting Puerto Rico's heritage and self-governance is critical for any oversight function to be accepted and effective. If that core tenant is not observed, it will be impossible to adopt and sustain sufficient reforms over the long-term. At the same time, the oversight board should have sufficient powers to assure stakeholders that necessary reforms will be implemented.

THE ADMINISTRATION'S RESPONSE TO THE CRISIS

I will conclude by sharing more information on the Administration's response to the crisis.

Secretary Lew created a dedicated team within Treasury to evaluate Puerto Rico's fiscal outlook and share our expertise with the officials that oversee the Commonwealth's economic policies.

Since its formation, the team has visited Puerto Rico regularly to review Puerto Rico's financial data, offer our perspectives on how other entities have managed through similar crises, and discuss options Puerto Rico could pursue to restore economic growth. We interact regularly with the Governor, members of Puerto Rico's legislature, business leaders and workers as well as creditors. We also speak every day with the officials managing Puerto Rico's fiscal response.

In December, Congress also provided Treasury with the authority to offer technical assistance to Puerto Rico in specialized areas such as revenue collections and budgeting. Since then, we have worked with the Commonwealth to assess its capacity to receive technical assistance, identified high priority needs, and already deployed the first set of technical advisors.

Technical assistance, while necessary, is not a solution for Puerto Rico's fiscal challenges. These tools will benefit the financial structure of the Island in the long-term, but Puerto Rico needs an immediate solution to address its unstable financial outlook today.

The White House National Economic Council and Treasury are also leading the Administration-wide effort to address the immediate crisis and take steps to put in place a foundation for economic growth and recovery. This longstanding effort includes the support of the White House Task Force on Puerto Rico, the Office of Management and Budget, the Department of Health and Human Services, the Department of Justice, and a number of other Federal agencies that interact with Puerto Rico on critical needs. Through this effort, the Administration has already facilitated significant steps to strengthen the Island's healthcare delivery, improve infrastructure, and attract new job-creating investments.

Secretary Lew also traveled to Puerto Rico last month as part of the Administration's continued engagement with Puerto Rico, meeting with elected officials, labor and community leaders, and the business community on the Island. The trip was the first of five scheduled visits by Cabinet Secretaries to Puerto Rico, with more to come.

And, today, Secretary Foxx is in San Juan to sign an agreement with Puerto Rico's transportation authority. The agreement will provide Puerto Rico with technical assistance to accelerate $400 million of available infrastructure funds. During their visits, Cabinet Secretaries will work with Puerto Rico on the reforms needed to support growth, including transportation infrastructure investments, strengthening primary and secondary education, expanding agricultural production, and addressing the impacts of drought.

While the Administration will continue to implement actions that strengthen Puerto Rico, Congressional action is needed for Puerto Rico to fully address its crisis.

CONCLUSION

Puerto Rico lacks the tools required to resolve this crisis on its own. The question is not whether the Commonwealth will restructure its debts, but when, and at what cost to the 3.5 million Americans on the Island.

The Administration will leave no stone unturned and bring all of our capabilities to bear in support of our fellow citizens in Puerto Rico. But only Congress can provide the comprehensive solution Puerto Rico requires.

There is a justifiable expectation the Administration and Congress will work together and that Congress will ultimately act as it has always done when there is a crisis that affects Americans. Our fellow citizens in Puerto Rico expect Congress to do what is necessary to stem the crisis, to protect the people of Puerto Rico, and to allow the economy to return to a path toward growth.

We look forward to working with this committee on legislation that will protect our fellow citizens in Puerto Rico.

———

The CHAIRMAN. Thank you. I appreciate your testimony. I will now turn to questions from the committee.

We only have one witness, I was a little bit flexible with that. I am not going to be flexible with you all. You have 5 minutes for the questioning period here.

And to try to get everyone—this is actually Vice Chairman Lummis' suggestion—let's go to the beginning of our dais, and see if we can get some other questions from those people who usually have to sit here for a long time.

So, Mr. MacArthur, I am going to turn to you for the first questions.

Mr. MACARTHUR. Thank you, Mr. Chairman. And, Mr. Weiss, I appreciate you being here. This is, obviously, an extremely complicated and difficult issue that we face.

You made a distinction between the territories and the states with regard to bankruptcy and fiscal issues in your opening statement. I just want to make sure I understand you. Are you suggesting that a Chapter 9-like mechanism should be extended to Puerto Rico?

Mr. WEISS. We are proposing a legislative act pursuant to the territorial clause of the Constitution, and it is meant to be customized to the unique conditions that face Puerto Rico in this crisis.

It is not necessarily a version of Chapter 9, or an expanded version of Chapter 9. It is, rather, a pairing of oversight authorities and restructuring, which would travel together. So, no, it is a legislative act that is tailored to the territories.

Mr. MACARTHUR. Would it allow territories like Puerto Rico to avoid debts in ways similar to how municipalities, cities, and such avoid debt repayment in Chapter 9? Would it act in similar ways?

Mr. WEISS. Well, our proposal is that Puerto Rico would have the option to elect oversight, and that, as I said earlier, there should be an initial period of negotiation. But if that negotiation fails because of the enormous complexity of the debt stock and the competing claims, or if that negotiation fails to get all of the creditors to agree to the same terms, then it would go to a court of supervision which would adjust the remaining claims.

Mr. MACARTHUR. You just used the phrase Puerto Rico electing oversight. What powers would you see this independent authority having? And, would you see them only having these authorities if the Puerto Rico legislature agreed to give them these authorities?

Mr. WEISS. Well, the authorities would be enacted by Congress, the U.S. Federal Congress. But, it is our judgment that to be effective, we need to achieve two objectives. First, the authorities need to be respectful of the Commonwealth's self-governance. We think anything that falls short of that will fail.

At the same time, there needs to be enough strength in the oversight to remedy what is a long history of fiscal mismanagement, inadequate financial disclosure, and to ensure that in the initial restructuring of debts, all stakeholders would be assured that, over time, promises would be kept, needed reforms would be made, and that the Commonwealth would ultimately emerge from this authority with a sustainable level of debt and a real economic future.

Mr. MACARTHUR. I understand the aspiration. But the reality on the ground is there is this much money available and this much obligation and expectation by a lot of different people. So it is quite conceivable to me that the legislature in Puerto Rico might not elect to have the degree of oversight that Congress believes is necessary to solve this.

I want to be clear. I want you to be clear. Do you believe that we should have an oversight board that Congress gives powers in exchange for the debt relief that is necessary? Do you believe that the Puerto Rico legislature should have the right to elect that before that power is given?

Mr. WEISS. Congressman, thank you for the question. It is something that we would look to work on with this committee to craft in a way that would be effective.

It is our judgment that, given the gravity of the crisis in Puerto Rico, the benefits of this authority would lead to its being broadly accepted if it is properly crafted.

Mr. MACARTHUR. I don't have time for you to answer this, unless we have another round of questions. But if we do not get back to it, I would like you to respond in writing. I think it is important that we consider the implication on the broader bond markets if we allow a Chapter 9-like restructuring in Puerto Rico, and what that does to bondholders throughout the whole municipal bond market.

Mr. WEISS. I would be——

Mr. MACARTHUR. I would appreciate it—you don't have time to answer, my time is expired, but I would like to hear at some point what you believe the potential consequences are elsewhere. I yield back.

The CHAIRMAN. No, you owe me 11 seconds.

Mr. MACARTHUR. All right.

The CHAIRMAN. Mr. Grijalva.

Mr. GRIJALVA. Thank you, Mr. Chairman. And thank you, Mr. Weiss. I want to thank you for a very comprehensive written statement. It answered many questions that have been raised about the proposal you outlined in your oral testimony.

That being said, I have one remaining question. What is your plan B? How do we plan on averting a humanitarian crisis in Puerto Rico that you warn of, if your efforts to get Congress to act do not pan out? Is there a plan B?

Mr. WEISS. The only durable comprehensive solution to this crisis is for the Administration to work together with Congress to implement oversight with restructuring. Anything that falls short of that will not provide a durable remedy, in our judgment. We have spent the better part of a year analyzing every option that is available to us, to the Administration, or to Congress, and restructuring paired with oversight is really the arrangement which provides the best chance for Puerto Rico to emerge from this crisis.

Mr. GRIJALVA. Mr. Weiss, it has been suggested that bankruptcy for Puerto Rico is a huge mistake, that what the island needs is to reduce spending and simply repay its obligation. How does Treasury feel about that assessment? Do you agree, as others have suggested, that granting bankruptcy or restructuring authority to Puerto Rico would be changing the rules in the middle of the game, two issues that have come up previously?

Mr. WEISS. Thank you. Two questions which I would like to take in order.

Mr. GRIJALVA. Yes.

Mr. WEISS. I think the second one comes back to the question of the Congressman, as well.

As to the first question, the Puerto Rican people have already confronted a financial crisis that has gone on for the better part of a decade. The Commonwealth has lost access to traditional municipal bond markets 2½ years ago, and today has access to no financing, is out of cash.

And we are really confronted with a choice between a cascading series of defaults and intensifying litigation that, in our judgment, could last a decade, or an orderly framework under clear Federal guidelines that would permit the Commonwealth to negotiate with all of its stakeholders in order to emerge with a sustainable level of debt.

When one analyzes this from a market perspective, and you know, we at Treasury have, obviously, given this a lot of thought. It is our judgment that the best of the two options, a disorderly default that cascades over time or an orderly framework designed by Congress and federally mandated, that of those two options, it does not come close. The best thing for municipal bond markets is for this crisis to be brought to an orderly resolution. Traditional investors tell us this all the time.

Just yesterday, one of the most prominent municipal bond investors issued a report in which they said, "Without Federal action that offers oversight and restructuring, there is a risk of a decade of litigation and default, that the economy, already strained, would be weakened, and that it would be far preferable—and they say this as a municipal bond investor—for there to be order restored in Puerto Rico, and that there would be limited, if any, precedential spillover effects to the broader municipal market." We share that conclusion.

Mr. GRIJALVA. So, essentially, for Puerto Rico to survive and begin a renewal of their economy and deal with the action on those two areas, the oversight and the restructuring by Congress, mandated by Congress, is essential in moving forward in any way. Is that the gist of everything?

Mr. WEISS. We think that that is a necessary condition to restart growth, that there will be other measures needed in such vital areas as health care and incentives to work, and potentially others, but that if we want to arrest the crisis and create that opportunity, we need to start with oversight and restructuring.

Mr. GRIJALVA. Thank you.

The CHAIRMAN. Thank you.

Mr. WEISS. Thank you.

The CHAIRMAN. Mr. LaHood.

Mr. LAHOOD. Thank you, Mr. Chairman. And, Mr. Weiss, thank you for being here today, and for your testimony.

In your opening remarks there, I did not hear you talk much about how we get the private sector flourishing in Puerto Rico. When you look at the statistics with Puerto Rico—and one theme is really the poor business climate there, the barriers in place that have kind of been systemic there for a while—and I know you talked about the debt restructuring and the oversight, but in terms of how we change the culture there to get the private sector to flourish—I mean, you read about the regulations, whether it is enforcing contracts, the tax system, registering property.

Traditionally, Puerto Rico ranks very, very low, in terms of doing that. And I know the debt is part of that, but looking at whether we engage in this legislation, how do we reduce those barriers? Because it seems to be a direct correlation to the hemorrhaging of people, talent, and opportunities out of Puerto Rico to Orlando, Florida, and lots of other places. If we do not have that business structure reform, how is this going to work?

Mr. WEISS. We share your frustration on this point in the sense that there is an enormous amount of capital, in our judgment private-sector capital, that is ready to invest in Puerto Rico, be that in alternative sources of energy generation or be that in modernizing the electricity grid, which is terribly out of date.

The problem we run into time and time again when we talk to investors is that this uncertainty that the economy faces makes it impossible for private-sector participants to invest and plan over any meaningful time horizon.

So, I am not saying it will solve all the problems, but if we do not clean the debt structure and put this economy back on a track toward a sustainable amount of debt—right now, 35 percent of central government revenues are being spent on debt service. Outmigration has more than doubled in the past 2 years. Unless we can stem this tide and create a base for the government and the private sector to plan against, we are deeply concerned that all of that third-party capital will never come into the island.

Mr. LAHOOD. Assuming that you get what you want in this, what assurance do you have when it comes to those other things I mentioned that are really prohibitive measures to investing, whether it is the issues with contracts, registering property, taxes—when you say there is a flood of private-sector investment that is ready to come in, if none of those things are changed, why would they come in?

Mr. WEISS. Congressman, again, the biggest barrier to investment today is the uncertainty and crisis that the economy is facing.

As to the regulatory aspects that you are referring to, again, it comes back to a key component of our proposal, which is to say that we believe that it is for the Puerto Rican legislature and the Governor to identify the reforms that are needed, the elected representatives to identify the reforms that are needed, structurally. But we think it is equally important—and that private capital would value this—that the oversight board make sure that those reforms identified by duly-elected representatives are implemented.

There is an enormous problem of over-promising and underdelivering that has gone on for many years in Puerto Rico. In our

18

judgment, marrying the self-governance of elected officials with the oversight of an independent board is exactly the structure which can remedy this.

Mr. LAHOOD. Two follow-up questions. Are there currently any existing Federal laws that, in your view, prohibit the ability to attract private investment in Puerto Rico? That is first. Then, second, are you confident in the legislators in Puerto Rico that these reforms that are necessary and needed are going to get done?

Mr. WEISS. On the first point, by far the biggest barrier to investment in Puerto Rico—and we have spoken with capital providers, we have spoken with potential lenders, and we have spoken with companies which would be interested in participating, for example, in the energy sector—the first and most important aspect is that the economy needs to be stabilized. No one invests in an economy that is in free fall. We need to stabilize the economy.

Second, the Puerto Rican legislature and Governor are in an election cycle—there will be a new governor. The current governor has said he will not run. And those duly-elected representatives will identify what it is that needs to be done.

But this interaction with an——

The CHAIRMAN. Mr. Weiss, I need to cut it off here, I am sorry.

Let me just give warning to all Members. We are slipping over time here, and that just cannot happen. So, in deference to the witness, if you are going to ask a question, give him enough time to answer it. If we run over the 5-minute mark, I am going to cut you off. So a lot of yes/no answers from here on in.

Mr. Pierluisi.

Mr. PIERLUISI. Yes. This——

Mr. WEISS. No.

[Laughter.]

Mr. PIERLUISI. No, no, I will be fine.

The CHAIRMAN. Yes.

Mr. PIERLUISI. At this juncture, I am convinced that Puerto Rico cannot either cut its way out of this crisis or tax its way out of this crisis. The only way out for Puerto Rico is to grow out of this crisis.

The critical obstacle to being able to do that is that Puerto Rico is about to default in a massive scale on hundreds of millions of dollars, if not billions of dollars, on payments it owes to bondholders all over America. So, that is what we should not ignore here.

We can have an independent board. I am running for governor. If anybody should be opposing that board, it is Yours Truly, and I don't. You have to understand that the board can come up with all kinds of recommendations and guidance for Puerto Rico to follow, but we have to address first things first. We need to make sure that Puerto Rico has the necessary access to the markets to comply with its payment obligations in the markets.

Creditors and the government have not been able to engage. I am not going to get into the blame game, but it has not happened. So, we need to incentivize that. One way we can incentivize that is by giving the board the necessary restructuring authority to promote negotiation. It could be mediation. And, short of that, or that failing, then providing for a fair restructuring deal for all parties involved.

That is the proposal I believe Treasury is putting forth. We can tinker with it, but let's not lose sight of the fact that Puerto Rico is not going to be able to grow if it has no access to the markets, if its reputation is stained in the markets. You need access to the markets to operate the government.

And last—and then I will let you react, Mr. Weiss—keep in mind that these are American citizens. That is why I say we cannot keep increasing taxes down there. That would be toxic for the business sector. And we cannot cut away and affect essential services, because you know what is going to happen? My constituents are going to hop on a plane like they have been doing, come to the mainland, and that is going to make it impossible for the economy of Puerto Rico to grow.

That is why this is complex. We need to be fair, and I would like you, Mr. Weiss, to react to my comment.

Mr. WEISS. Congressman, you have been a leader on this topic and have introduced many potential legislative acts that would make a difference, and we have greatly appreciated our work with you.

I want to highlight something you said, which is that if you go to Puerto Rico and you spend time with the Americans who live in Puerto Rico—and I said this in my opening remarks—there is actual fear of the future. The payments which are coming due—$400 million on May 1, $2 billion on July 1—no one knows where the money will come from to fund those payments. And, faced with this enormous fiscal uncertainty, with diminishing health care provision, with no jobs available on the island, Puerto Ricans are leaving.

And it is the young, working-age Puerto Ricans who are leaving for the most part, and they are joining us on the mainland. On the mainland they find that they have access to jobs, opportunities for employment, a future for their children, and better health care. What that is doing is dramatic. I should mention there is 2.5 percent annually in out-migration of working-age citizens. Ten years from now, if we do nothing to stop this, there will be no revenue base against which to construct a viable economy.

So, we fully agree with you, Congressman, that we need to take these actions today, and that the time for action has really already passed.

Mr. PIERLUISI. Thank you. I yield back.

The CHAIRMAN. Thank you very much. You owe me 11, you get 10, so we will go from there.

Mr. Hice, you came in a bit late. Are you prepared for questions right now?

Dr. HICE. Yes, sir.

The CHAIRMAN. Mr. Hice, you are recognized.

Dr. HICE. Thank you, Mr. Chairman. I appreciate this very important hearing that we are having.

Mr. Weiss, I agree with my colleague that the way out of this, obviously, is growth. Puerto Rico has at times sought to become a party to various U.S. income tax treaties, and yet the Treasury Department has turned down these efforts. Given the dire circumstances, would you support or do you favor a change in policy in this regard?

Mr. WEISS. Congressman, the immediate problem is the unsustainable debt. There is nothing that can be done with respect to tax policy or even health care, as dire as that is, that will remedy the fact that $70 billion of debt against a $70 billion economy that consumes 35 percent of revenues has to be reset.

Dr. HICE. I understand that. But my question is, would you support a change in policy?

Mr. WEISS. As to the opportunities to promote growth, once that has been done and there is an oversight board in place, we would be happy to work with you and your staff about potential solutions that could attract jobs, that could incentivize——

Dr. HICE. All right. You are going far beyond yes/no answers with this. It was a relatively simple question.

It is becoming clear to me and to many others that the emerging consensus around Congress is that there should probably be a control board, much less consensus regarding Federal bankruptcy protection.

You may or may not be familiar. Do you know whether or not the District of Columbia got Chapter 9 bankruptcy protection 20 years ago?

Mr. WEISS. The District of Columbia was a fiscal crisis, as opposed to a debt crisis. Mayor Williams has testified——

Dr. HICE. Again, that is not my question. Did they get bankruptcy protection?

Mr. WEISS. They got a fiscal control board, because that attacked the problem they had. Here we have an economy drowning in debt, which requires restructuring along with oversight.

Dr. HICE. That is true. Do you believe a control board of some sort could be effective in reorganizing Puerto Rico's finances without filing Chapter 9 bankruptcy?

Mr. WEISS. To be clear, we are not proposing Chapter 9 or any new chapter of the code. We are proposing a territorial act, which would allow for restructuring authorities, only by acting through and with an oversight board. It is our judgment that that is the only combination that can produce a durable solution.

We do not want to be sitting back here July 2 or July 5, after Puerto Rico has failed to pay $2 billion, including $800 million of constitutionally prioritized debt, which would provoke a constitutional crisis and litigation. Our interest is in designing a permanent solution.

And it just has to be said, yes, there has been fiscal mismanagement. Yes, there is need for oversight. But this debt has to be reduced.

Dr. HICE. It does.

Mr. WEISS. It needs to be done fairly.

Dr. HICE. Let's go on, you are taking my time. The question was do you believe a control board would be helpful, and you have still not answered that question. Yes or no?

Mr. WEISS. We believe an oversight board coupled with restructuring would be effective.

Dr. HICE. OK. Let's shift gears a little bit. You talk about restructuring. Before any restructuring takes place, wouldn't it be good to have some real numbers, such as something that would come from an audit of the finances, which has not taken place now in quite some time?

Mr. WEISS. We agree that the fiscal transparency is totally inadequate. One affirmative obligation we would put on the oversight board, if Congress agreed, would be actual powers to make sure that the financial reporting systems are integrated, modernized, and that audits are produced on a timely basis. We think that that is necessary for all stakeholders—debtors, investors——

Dr. HICE. Mr. Weiss, you ramble a lot. These are not complicated questions. Can we expect an audit? Yes or no.

Mr. WEISS. Absolutely.

Dr. HICE. OK. What kind of progress is being made on that? At what point can we expect an audit?

Mr. WEISS. Our understanding is that there has been a draft audit released, and that the auditors have announced that they need 2 months to review it.

It should be no surprise that an entity in distress has difficulty getting going concern opinions for its subchapters. This is the set of issues that Puerto Rico is facing. It is a distressed entity.

Dr. HICE. Time has expired. I would appreciate more yes/no answers, direct answers, but I yield back. Thank you, sir.

The CHAIRMAN. Ms. Bordallo.

Ms. BORDALLO. Thank you, Mr. Chairman, and to our witness, Mr. Weiss, for being here today.

The situation in Puerto Rico compels action, and I am very glad we are finally here today to discuss it. I thank the Administration for including the other territories in their proposals to address some of Puerto Rico's most pressing issues, and I urge leadership to also consider including the other territories as they draft legislation.

While our challenges are nowhere near as serious as Puerto Rico's, our territories do face challenges. I believe the inclusion of territories would avert similar crises in the future. To that end, I introduced legislation that would give the Government of Guam flexibility in extending Social Security to employees of the government. These employees are currently not a part of the system. Our retirement fund has identified the current pension system is fiscally unsustainable. So, we must be proactive to address these problems.

I also hope that the committee can consider the smaller territories as they look to other fixes for Puerto Rico, such as cover-over for the EITC and improving the FMAC for Medicaid. With that, I have a few questions for Mr. Weiss.

To what extend did the failure of the Puerto Rico pension program contribute to their current economic crisis? And do you agree that steps should be taken to prevent a similar situation in the other territories? If you could, make your answers short.

Mr. WEISS. We are deeply concerned about the pensions in Puerto Rico—330,000 current and retired Puerto Rican employees, public employees, depend on it. The pensions are, essentially, unfunded. We are this close to being under a regime where it is the Commonwealth itself which would have to fund pension payments.

Ms. BORDALLO. What about the other territories?

Mr. WEISS. As to the other territories, we would be happy to work with you to look into the particulars around Guam.

Ms. BORDALLO. All right. I do appreciate that the Treasury included the smaller territories in the debt-restructuring proposal. However, was there a consideration of including the smaller territories in the other proposals, like cover-over for EITC and improving the FMAC for the Medicaid program?

I would note that the President's budget includes requests from HHS that would improve our FMAC over time. An improved FMAC and cover-over of EITC would free up significant local funding and put us on a fiscally sustainable path. Do you agree with this?

Mr. WEISS. Again, our proposals are with respect to the territories as a whole, and we would be prepared to work with you on the particulars of Guam and the other territories.

Ms. BORDALLO. So then, Mr. Weiss, I would like to make it very clear. Do you agree that inclusion of the territories in the Puerto Rico relief package would help to avert similar crises in the territories in the future?

Mr. WEISS. We would be happy to come meet with you and discuss the ways in which that would be possible with the appropriate staff.

Ms. BORDALLO. Thank you. And, Mr. Chairman, I go on record in full support of solving the Puerto Rico financial crisis and, of course, the inclusion of the other territories in this legislation. I yield back.

The CHAIRMAN. Now I owe you a minute-and-a-half. Sheesh.

[Laughter.]

The CHAIRMAN. Mr. Duncan, I realize I have you in No Man's Land. Regardless of where I start, you are going to be last. But I understand that you have another commitment you have to be at right now, so let me recognize you for 5 minutes for questions.

Mr. DUNCAN. Thank you, Mr. Chairman. I appreciate what you are doing. I have been a freshman Member and have not had an opportunity to ask questions in the past, so thank you on behalf of——

The CHAIRMAN. Now you are a more advanced Member that does not have the chance to ask questions.

[Laughter.]

Mr. DUNCAN. Thank you. I do have John Kerry in Foreign Affairs, and that is an important topic for me.

I want to follow the line of Mr. Hice from Georgia, in that Puerto Rico has not issued an audited financial statement and they won't until April, according to the Governor—and there is a letter in Reuters over that. Paul Ryan has requested we take action by March, but we are not going to have an audited financial statement until April. So, I think Congress is flying blind, and I do not believe we should take any action until we truly know an audited financial picture of the Commonwealth.

But I will say this, following the gentleman's line earlier about bankruptcy and access to capital markets, I believe bankruptcy will actually close access to financial markets for Puerto Rico for an indeterminate number of years and that would be detrimental, I think, to rebuilding and some of the quality of life issues.

When I study this and I look at the amount of money that may be available for debt service, there are a lot of different figures thrown around. So, Mr. Weiss, I would ask what you believe the amount of money available for debt service, in terms of percentage of the budget, would be for 2016?

Mr. WEISS. As I mentioned earlier, the debt service figures are approximately a third of central government revenues. The Commonwealth itself has proposed a voluntary exchange offer——

Mr. DUNCAN. So, you are sticking to that 42 percent number that has been touted by a lot of different sources?

Mr. WEISS. Depending on the year, it is about a third, or higher than a third.

Mr. DUNCAN. I realize that some of the government borrowing and loans and other things cannot be used to pay debt service, and that is common. But those can be used to provide for other services that the government provides. That frees up money that is not being used in these calculations that is available for debt service.

I am going to ask to submit for the record testimony to the Senate Committee on the Judiciary, Orrin Hatch's committee, by Carlos Colón-De-Armas, Mr. Chairman. I believe with him that that number is closer to 16 percent. So, I think we need to get a better handle on what monies are available for Puerto Rico for true debt service, and what monies are available for Puerto Rico for public services other than debt service, so that we can truly compare apples to apples and not be an alarmist and say that only 42 percent of the total available resources for Puerto Rico are obligated.

Mr. Chairman, I don't have a lot of questions. I wanted to make those points, and I do want to provide this for the record because I think it is so important. With that, I will yield back.

The CHAIRMAN. Thank you.

Ms. Tsongas.

Ms. TSONGAS. Thank you, Mr. Chairman, and thank you, Mr. Weiss, for being here with us today. This is a complicated issue. I appreciate your insights and the deep thought that the Administration has given to the most productive way forward.

And just to sort of frame this in a slightly different path, I think what happens in Puerto Rico, as you have said, at the very least in sort of the out-migration that is taking place, will come and be part of our country. And my district is very reflective of that. One in five of my constituents identify as Hispanic or Latino, and 40 percent of them are from Puerto Rico. So many of them have friends and family who still live there, and they have seen first-hand the devastating effects that the 10-year recession and the debt crisis have had on the island. This is something that those of us who represent significant Puerto Rican populations have to take very seriously, what the most productive way forward is.

A lot of the debate is whether a voluntary agreement—or really, I think the crux of the debate is whether voluntary agreements alone are a sufficient way forward, versus whether you need to have a restructuring option at hand, as well.

And again, you have given some testimony to this effect. But, I would like your thoughts as to the many complexities of the voluntary path, and solely that path, without the restructuring option at hand. And I will give you some time to answer that.

Mr. WEISS. Thank you, Congresswoman. That is the right way to frame the question in our judgment.

So today, without any tools to restructure the debt, Puerto Rico is faced with 20 different creditor classes and 18 different issuers with competing claims.

On December 1, just to take one example, the Governor decided to not pay three debts in order to pay other debts. This has immediately prompted litigation by the three creditors who were not paid. As this unfolds and the maturities come that Congressman Pierluisi was referring to, this will magnify and intensify.

There are really two major problems in a voluntary discussion. First is that there is no stay on litigation. So, litigation as to priority of payment, as to eligibility for any particular agreement, will ensue. Second is that there is no way to reach agreement with a majority of creditors in any given class and know that the minority creditors will go along. And there have been many examples of this around the world.

And we do worry that the compounding effects of litigation and an inability to conclude agreements with any creditor class could turn a purely voluntary process into a decade-long crisis. So that restructuring authority that you mentioned is really what is needed at the back end.

We support an initial period of voluntary discussions. We think that those voluntary discussions can only succeed with this kind of back-end authority.

Ms. TSONGAS. What would be the impact on the citizens of Puerto Rico if—and the lengthy process of a solely voluntary way forward—what would be the impact on the citizens?

Mr. WEISS. The Governor has already been forced to curtail services, as I mentioned in my opening remarks. As the debt payments become larger, as the most senior debt becomes due, $800 million of constitutionally-protected debt on July 1, the decisions become more difficult and the litigation becomes more severe.

And this is not lost on the citizens of Puerto Rico. And you have them in your district, but I can tell you that our fellow citizens in Puerto Rico are acutely aware of the kind of trade-offs that the government could face if these maturities come due, litigation builds, and the services need to be traded off against constitutionally-protected debt.

Ms. TSONGAS. Thank you for your testimony, and I yield back.

The CHAIRMAN. Thank you.

Mr. Zinke.

Mr. ZINKE. Thank you, Mr. Chairman, and thank you for holding what appears to be a bipartisan effort to fix the problem.

It is interesting that Montana is about a million people, Puerto Rico is about three times the size. And we are not a territory, we are a state. But clearly I looked at the Constitution—and I will quote—"The Congress shall have the power to dispose and make all needful rules and regulations respecting the territory or the property belonging to the United States." Clearly, Congress has the power.

And to your point, in the 1990s, Congress did look at Washington, DC, and the District, and there seems to be a great bit of difference between the two, particularly in the debt.

And as I look at it, the discussion is on the control board, what power? On one side you have an advisory board. On the other side controlling every aspect of the Puerto Rican Commonwealth.

I guess my question to you is what do you believe are the core explicit powers that the Federal oversight should have?

Mr. WEISS. I am going to give you a couple of examples of this, and thank you for the question.

We totally agree that an advisory board is insufficient, and we totally agree that a takeover of the Commonwealth through direct control will be ineffective.

So, in that middle space the concept is that the elected officials of Puerto Rico would retain their rights to tax, spend, and govern the Commonwealth. They are closest to it, and there is enormous complexity in the existing economy. But the oversight board would ensure that whatever promises are made, those promises are adhered to.

They would provide guardrails on the economy such that, for example, if there is an initial plan to restructure the debt based on 5 years of projections and the first budget comes up and that budget is not consistent with that 5-year plan, then the oversight board should get involved and enter into discussions such that that budget conforms to the 5-year plan.

If into that year actual performance is short of budget, again, the oversight board should make it known that there needs to be action. But we do not believe in an oversight board deciding which taxes to adjust or which expenses to cut. Those are decisions that need to remain with the Commonwealth.

Mr. ZINKE. Where would you place a priority of an independent audit?

Mr. WEISS. If this is where you are going, we agree that we think there needs to be an ability to audit independently at the level of the oversight board, and to produce revenue forecasts that are independent. What this does is it respects the political process of the elected officials in the Commonwealth, but also creates a second board which is outside of the political process and will last through election cycles, and which will produce credible, independent revenue statements.

One thing I mentioned earlier is, we also think that that board has a role to play—there have been a lot of comments on audits and financial systems and such, which we agree are antiquated. That is fixable. And that oversight board should be charged with making sure that that gets fixed.

Mr. ZINKE. I look to my colleague's point about the economy. I don't know a lot about Puerto Rico, but I have looked into—a lot of the baseline economy is the ability to produce power at a rate that is reliable and affordable. If we are going to look at manufacturing, certainly that has to be a part of it.

And my understanding is the power plant, the structure of it gets their fuel load at an excessive price, and there has not been a lot of investment into that power plant. If we are going to look at driving the economy as far as jobs, that power plant has to be part of it. Is there any idea how to address that portion of it?

Mr. WEISS. You know, we agree. The power generation in Puerto Rico is really oil and coal, very little else. But the good news here is there is serious appetite on the part of companies and investors to invest in Puerto Rico to modernize the sources of power generation.

So, we do believe that the private sector has an important role to play. If we fix the level of debt and we create durable fiscal governance, we think private capital will come.

Mr. ZINKE. Thank you, Mr. Chairman, and I yield back.

Mr. HUFFMAN. Thank you, Mr. Chair. I will yield the balance of my time to my colleague from Puerto Rico, Mr. Pierluisi.

Mr. PIERLUISI. Thank you. Mr. Chairman, I will respect the time constraints so that we keep going forward expeditiously.

Mr. Weiss, at a recent event you stated that there is no question that status is vitally important when looking at the situation, the fiscal and economic crisis that Puerto Rico is facing.

And I should say that back in 2010, when Congress was considering and enacted the Affordable Care Act, we had a great opportunity to provide parity, equal treatment to all the territories under the Medicaid program. I fought for that; my colleagues, the delegates for the territories, fought for that; and my fellow Members of Congress from Puerto Rico fought for that. Unfortunately, the Congress fell short. Because now Puerto Rico faces a very serious cliff, in terms of the lack of funding it has under the Medicaid program.

Let me explain this. It is not only affecting our ability to provide adequate care for the medically indigent. It also exerts an incredible fiscal pressure on the territorial government. I give that as an example. We should do much better there.

I would like you, Mr. Weiss, to elaborate on this point: ways in which, apart from creating a board and providing a fair and debt restructuring mechanism, ways in which Congress can assist Puerto Rico while dealing with the disparities we face as a territory.

Mr. WEISS. Congressman, we believe that status has played a role in the development of the fiscal crisis over many, many years in Puerto Rico. And we believe that status should be determined by the people in Puerto Rico in a process, and we have supported that in the President's last budgets. But, why are we proposing restructuring authorities, EITC, and Medicaid funding as part of our comprehensive plan? Well, it is because the Commonwealth status has not afforded it equitable treatment in those three areas.

That said, this crisis is upon us today. And today, in order for Puerto Rico to have any long-term future under any status, we do need to act in the two ways which I have mentioned earlier: oversight with restructuring authorities.

Mr. PIERLUISI. I yield back.

Mr. HUFFMAN. Thank you, Mr. Chairman.

The CHAIRMAN. Mr. Graves.

Mr. GRAVES. Thank you, Mr. Chairman, and Mr. Weiss, thank you for being here. Your testimony has been very informative, so thank you.

A question for you in following up on previous questions from my neighbor, here. The Puerto Rican Constitution, the territory's Constitution, as I understand, prioritizes debt over all other expenditures. Obviously, the whole issue on balancing autonomy with proper fiscal reform and oversight is going to be an interesting balance.

It is my understanding that last year when legislation was brought up that was going to change the Constitution to provide for more flexibility there, that the Governor opposed it, and that some of the legislators indicated their opposition, as well. Changing the Constitution, as I understand it, would require a two-thirds vote in the legislature, and be presented to the folks in Puerto Rico under referendum.

How do you balance the autonomy issue with, as I hear you saying—and I do not want to put words in your mouth—but as I hear you saying, effectively coming in and restructuring their debt to where the oversight board would have the ability to trump the Constitution?

Mr. WEISS. Again, our basic philosophy on this is that the restructuring should include all of the debt, that all of the debt is part of the unsustainable $70 billion. But we are not proposing a one-size-fits-all solution. So, we are not saying that the GO debt, which has a Puerto Rican constitutional priority, or some of the revenue bonds which have a claim on certain streams, that those all need to be treated equally. This is not one-size-fits-all.

So, what we can do, working together, is to design a restructuring authority whereby everybody is part of the discussion, but that there is a differentiated treatment per existing priorities and plans——

Mr. GRAVES. I have two other questions. I appreciate the thorough answer, and certainly want to get those, but being respectful of time here, very quickly, I will perhaps ask it this way. Is it your view that the territory clause in the U.S. Constitution trumps the prioritization of expenditure and debt clause in the Puerto Rican Constitution? Yes or no, please.

Mr. WEISS. We believe that we can construct this under the territorial clause.

Mr. GRAVES. Thank you. Next question. I was looking around at different options here, trying to understand this. Obviously, the issue as indicated by Mr. MacArthur earlier is a big concern. But in the past, Puerto Rico has issued tax anticipation notes in order to cover expenditures. This year, as I understand it, is the first year they have not issued an appropriate level to cover their expenses.

I understand that Mr. Pierluisi introduced legislation that would allow for the Federal Reserve Bank to acquire those notes. Have you all taken a position on that, and is that a component of what you see as being a long-term solution?

Mr. WEISS. We are not proposing that the Federal Government take on liabilities of the Commonwealth, or guarantee liabilities of the Commonwealth. They did lose access to that financing. It is not that they elected not to use it, they just did not have any access.

Mr. GRAVES. Another question—and I apologize, I had not had a chance to confirm this with the FERC, but it is my understanding—there were questions earlier that were brought up in regard to power. Obviously, the electricity prices there are significant compared to other parts of the United States. It is my understanding that there has been a gas terminal permit sitting on the FERC's desk for some period of time now that would provide for natural gas as a fuel stocked for electricity production, which again, when you look around the country, should provide significant relief in regard to rates.

I understand you are with Treasury, but just curious if that is on your radar, if that might be something that you are aware of?

Mr. WEISS. I am aware of it, but I would have to come back to you with the appropriate——

Mr. GRAVES. I would appreciate it. And again, I know you are not FERC.

Last question. I would actually like to follow up on Mr. MacArthur's question in regard to the bond market implications and precedent he was concerned about before. Forty-five seconds.

Mr. WEISS. I will just read a couple sentences from a report issued yesterday, and it will not take more than 20 seconds. This is from a Nuveen report issued yesterday. They are one of the largest traditional municipal bond investors, and they say that Puerto Rico—and I quote—"Without some form of bankruptcy, Puerto Rico is destined for years of litigation," and they say that "the restructuring provides greater value to creditors than maintaining the status quo, and that municipal investors rightly continue to differentiate among individual credits, and we see no reason this will change based on how Congress addresses Puerto Rico's situation." They see no spillover effects.

Mr. GRAVES. I yield back.

The CHAIRMAN. Thank you, appreciate that.

Mr. Clay, I think you are next.

Mr. CLAY. Thank you, Mr. Chairman, and thank you for conducting this hearing.

Mr. Weiss, a key element of the economic crisis in Puerto Rico is its impact on Puerto Rico health care and the system. Since passage of the ACA, the Secretary of HHS has used her existing discretionary authority to interpret most of the ACA as not applying to Puerto Rico and the territories. The territories, therefore, have no exchanges, no premium support, no coverage mandates, and no standards for health insurance plans. Yet the ACA's health insurance provider tax still applies to the territories.

Is it logical that the Administration uses its interpretive authority to relieve the territories of the benefits of the ACA, but it declines to use its interpretive authority to relieve them of the ACA's burdens? And do you foresee any relief for the island?

Mr. WEISS. I would like to come back to you with HHS personnel for the detail. I will give you a general point of view.

That ACA funding is a fiscal issue, in the end. The reason that we have proposed that Medicaid funding be included is that, as best we can tell, the allotment that Puerto Rico received at the time of the passage of the Affordable Care Act is going to be fully exhausted by March of 2018, if not sooner. So, this does need to be addressed urgently and it is a key component of our legislative package.

Mr. CLAY. Yes, and I am glad to hear that it is on your radar because, apparently, relief is needed.

One other question. We have heard that the consequences of a comprehensive debt restructuring for Puerto Rico would be far reaching and drive up the cost of borrowing for Puerto Rico in the long term, making sustainable economic development unlikely for the island. Will the enactment of debt restructuring for Puerto Rico result in increased borrowing costs for the island?

Mr. WEISS. Congressman, we believe just the opposite is true. We believe that this is a choice between no access to credit, which is Puerto Rico's current state; a cascading series of defaults; mounting litigation; and an inability to conclude a voluntary negotiation or an orderly process under Federal guidelines, such that there is an end to this fiscal crisis; and that there will be market access, as there has been in many regions that have gone through the same problem.

Mr. CLAY. So you don't see the costs being driven up for borrowing?

Mr. WEISS. We see no access without it.

Mr. CLAY. I see. I would like to yield to my colleague from Illinois, Mr. Gutierrez, the remaining time.

Mr. GUTIERREZ. Thank you, sir. Thank you so much. I appreciate the gentleman from Missouri yielding to me. And welcome, Mr. Weiss.

I just want to use this intervention to say that we have talked about fiscal mismanagement in Puerto Rico. You have talked about transparency in the budget. You said that promises need to be kept, reduce spending, and pay its obligations.

Where are the jobs? Where is the economic opportunity? Where is the possibility for the people of Puerto Rico? And I would simply suggest with the 50 seconds that I have that one of the things that was recommended is that—you said it, Mr. Weiss—visit, talk. You said you have been down there. When are we going to go down and listen to the people of Puerto Rico, and have a hearing there, front and center, so that we can hear what their dreams and aspirations are, so that we can see their lives?

It is good to go down to Puerto Rico to fill our campaign coffers and war chests, but we should also go to Puerto Rico not simply for partisan political reasons, to fill our campaign coffers, but we should go down there to fill our minds with their ideas, their aspirations, and their dreams. Because otherwise, I would suggest, Mr. Chairman—and I thank you—these hearings are simply seen as a way to humiliate the people of Puerto Rico, instead of lift them.

The CHAIRMAN. First, you came in late—I am going to give you a chance to catch your—let me go back to Mr. Labrador, you have been sitting here in No Man's Land again—and give you a chance to ask questions. Then we will catch up with some of the others who have been here.

Mr. LABRADOR. Thank you, Mr. Chairman. And I found that rather unfortunate, I think. That was the first time that partisanship has been brought up in this hearing today and Luis is a good friend. I was sad to hear that.

And I want to thank you. You have been going through a pretty good hearing today, a lot of really tough questions. And I don't

know you, but it sounds to me like you are at least trying to find
a solution to this problem, and I want to thank you for your efforts.
We do not agree on every one of your solutions, not everything that
you have said, but I can tell that the Administration—this is a
Republican speaking here—at least is acting in good faith, trying
to find a good solution to this problem that we all want to find a
solution for.

Mr. WEISS. Thank you, Congressman.

Mr. LABRADOR. Absolutely. I want to make something clear.
There has been a lot of talk about Chapter 9. You said in your
statement, and I think this has been missed, that Chapter 9 was
carefully designed for states in conformance with the 10th Amendment. So, in other words, you don't think Chapter 9 applies to this
situation. Is that correct?

Mr. WEISS. We don't think Chapter 9 solves the problem.

Mr. LABRADOR. OK, thank you. I just wanted to make that clear,
because I don't think that was heard by all those people that are
asking questions. Thank you.

You also stated that the plan proposed by the Administration includes a debt restructuring authority paired with fiscal oversight,
health care transformation, and tax incentives to reward work. I
want to speak to you for a few minutes about a few of these
elements.

First, the Administration has called for an independent Federal
oversight authority that respects Puerto Rican autonomy. Could
you explain what the Administration means when it says such authority must respect Puerto Rican autonomy?

Mr. WEISS. Thanks for the question. I tried to provide a partial
answer to this earlier. In essence, the elected government of Puerto
Rico, in our concept—and this is a principle—should continue to set
forth the major taxing and spending decisions that are necessary
to run the economy. No Federal authority can stand in the place
of these duly-elected officials to determine what is required.

But, due to the long-standing nature, and I have to go back to
the fiscal mismanagement which has taken place in the sense of
systematic under-estimating of expenses and over-forecasting of
revenues, investors have lost confidence in the numbers; the people
have lost confidence in the numbers. And we actually think getting
the numbers right makes a different here and can lead to greater
opportunity, greater investment, and greater job employment.

Mr. LABRADOR. Thank you——

Mr. WEISS. So, we see that the oversight board plays that
essential function.

Mr. LABRADOR. At the prior two hearings, I have highlighted the
importance of Puerto Rico to continue enacting necessary reforms
and negotiating voluntary debt restructuring agreements with their
creditors.

I am concerned because there was an article in *El Nuevo Día* on
February 18 that stated that Puerto Rican legislators will dam
up—they will stop, dam, d-a-m, up—the legislation if the legislation we craft seeks their ratification to impose Federal oversight
authority. The article is here.

So I want to know—I see the president of the Puerto Rican
Senate is behind you and he is nodding his head, but that is what

some people said in the article. I am concerned about that. Do you have any concerns that the Puerto Rican government would try to stop any kind of restructuring board or anything?

Mr. WEISS. May I cede my time to Senator Bhatia?

[Laughter.]

Mr. LABRADOR. I will speak with—I was glad to see him nodding his head no, because there are actually some statements in here that talk about that. It would be impossible, I think, for a reporter to get something wrong, because you know that never happens.

Do you think we can rely on the legislature to make the difficult decisions when some legislators are publicly vowing to oppose oversight authority?

Mr. WEISS. I think that the legislature does not fully understand what this oversight authority would consist of, nor do the people of Puerto Rico, for one simple reason: we have not presented it to them. I mean we are talking about it.

We are very appreciative of Chairman Bishop and his staff, and we are actually starting to put some details in place. But we will have to design this all the way into its detail, and convince the legislature and the people of Puerto Rico that it can be effective.

Mr. LABRADOR. OK. Finally, I also want to talk a little bit about promoting economic growth for Puerto Rico. I believe that the only way to get out of this crisis is to have fiscal promise by economic growth. Do you have concrete proposals for stimulating the economic growth?

Mr. WEISS. We do, and we are open to other ideas than the ones we have proposed. But we have looked at various levers. The Earned Income Tax Credit is one we think would be very effective.

Mr. LABRADOR. Thank you very much.

The CHAIRMAN. This is where you say, "Yes." And you should know in this part of the building you can cede to anyone except a Senator.

[Laughter.]

The CHAIRMAN. If you had been in the House, you would have been OK, but no, it doesn't work at all.

[Laughter.]

The CHAIRMAN. Mr. Beyer.

Mr. BEYER. Thank you, Mr. Chairman, and thank you, Mr. Weiss.

Representative Pierluisi spoke eloquently of the disparate treatment that Puerto Ricans have now under Federal law. And you talked about the oversight board, the fiscal restructuring. Can long-term fiscal stability come to Puerto Rico without addressing Medicare, Medicaid, EITC, and other stuff?

Mr. WEISS. We think long-term growth cannot. We think that long-term stability, the Number One important element is to restructure the debt and to do it with an independent oversight board. It is necessary, but not sufficient for growth. Other things have to be enacted for growth.

Mr. BEYER. I am told that, without really even looking at Medicare, you are going to be permanently structurally imbalanced for the long term, putting Puerto Rico back in the same position.

Mr. WEISS. Medicaid funding will run out by most estimates in March 2018. This does create a hole in the numbers that is considerable and it is why we have included it in our plan.

Mr. BEYER. You talked about $70 billion in debt, the declining population, and an aging population—2½ percent lost just last year. Is there any possible way to support $70 billion, even restructure, without significant haircuts to existing bondholders?

Mr. WEISS. No.

Mr. BEYER. So, it is imperative that some of the existing debt be written off in order to get it to a balanced——

Mr. WEISS. We would not prescribe what gets written off, what gets reprofiled, what gets restructured, and other means. But the absolute debt burden is clearly unsustainable, uncontroversially unsustainable.

Mr. BEYER. Yes. You talked about the oversight board, but also maintaining the local government autonomy. Can you talk about the dangers when there is not local government autonomy? And all of us are painfully aware of what happened in Flint recently, so——

Mr. WEISS. Well, we have with us a Congressman of Puerto Rican descent who is deeply familiar with the heritage and self-governing authorities of the Commonwealth. It would simply be rejected, in our judgment. A takeover of Puerto Rico by the Federal Government, we think, would be universally rejected. The reforms would never be implemented. So, it is simply not an option that Congress should consider.

Mr. BEYER. One question has been brought up a number of times, especially by my friends in the Majority, that the prospect of Puerto Rico really re-entering the bond market in a meaningful way after the write-offs, after whatever—if not Chapter 9, some type of fiscal restructuring. Are there examples in the past, other places, of successfully re-entering the credit markets after a restructuring?

Mr. WEISS. As I said, this is a tried-and-true combination. To pair oversight with restructuring has worked domestically many times. It has worked internationally many times. Cities like New York City, Washington, DC—notwithstanding that it was a fiscal, rather than debt crisis—and Philadelphia. Major companies, by the way, have gone through a restructuring and re-accessed markets. Markets inherently look forward, and what markets see when they look forward in Puerto Rico today is 10 years of cascading defaults, litigation, out-migration, and economic decline. No wonder Puerto Rico lost access 2½ years ago to traditional bond investors.

This needs to be stabilized. Once it is stabilized, and with the additional credibility afforded by independent oversight, it is our judgment that the credit markets will reopen.

Mr. BEYER. Thank you. Mr. Chair, I yield back.

The CHAIRMAN. Thank you.

Mr. Westerman.

Mr. WESTERMAN. Thank you, Mr. Chairman, and thank you, Mr. Weiss. I will reiterate the words from my colleague, Mr. Labrador. I appreciate your honest approach to this, and the Administration's efforts to try to come up with a real solution here——

Mr. WEISS. Thank you.

Mr. WESTERMAN [continuing]. And being transparent in identifying where the issues are.

As it has been noted, Puerto Rico has lost about 10 percent of its population and over 250,000 jobs in the last 10 years. Much of this is due to the lack of opportunities on the island, and also for the citizens' ability to move freely to the United States.

I know in some of the solutions you have proposed to try to help stem some of the out-migration, you have talked about extending programs like Medicaid and the Earned Income Tax Credit, to make it equal to what we have here in the states.

As I look at out-migration or migration into the states here, we see that there is a lot of data that shows that people move to states where there are more job opportunities. They may even move from states where there may be more Federal benefit programs to states where they have more job opportunities. I am wondering if in the analysis in coming up with these solutions, did you do any kind of a survey on when there is out-migration from Puerto Rico to the states, which states they are moving to, and what is attracting them to those states.

Mr. WEISS. Well, Congressman, it is definitely the case that we see Puerto Rican citizens moving for opportunity. I mean they are clearly moving for opportunity, because the vast majority are working age with families. These are not mainly retirees. They really see opportunity throughout the United States.

I would be happy to come back to you with a list of the states which are attracting the most Puerto Rican citizens, but it is really broad spread. It is everywhere from Florida, to New York, to Pennsylvania, to Texas, to Ohio. It is really quite a long list, and what that means is that the opportunity pretty much anywhere outside Puerto Rico is far greater than what is available in the Commonwealth.

Mr. WESTERMAN. I am guessing it would be similar to what we see here, where they are probably attracted to areas that have higher job growth and more job opportunities.

With that said, does the Administration have any proposals to attract growth on the island?

Mr. WEISS. We believe that there needs to be two phases to this. In the first phase, the debt needs to be restructured and there needs to be oversight. That will restore confidence in the numbers and it will stem the crisis. But in the second phase, there needs to be greater economic opportunity for the people in Puerto Rico, because we would like to not just see out-migration stop, but to see the many Puerto Ricans who live on the mainland have the opportunity to move back to Puerto Rico.

There are 5 million-plus Puerto Ricans in mainland United States versus 3.5 million on the island. Success here means that the flow moves in the other direction. So, yes, we have proposed an EITC. We think there are things the Puerto Rican legislature can do. As I mentioned earlier, we think there is a substantial role for industry and private capital, but none of those are going to get in place unless we stop this free fall of the crisis that we are in today.

Mr. WESTERMAN. And, as my colleagues from Montana and Louisiana talked about, energy issues on the island—I believe they pay approximately twice the cost per kilowatt hour for electricity as Americans pay, on average. Have there been any ideas or proposals to reform the energy sector on the island? Because obviously, low energy costs will help attract manufacturers and good jobs.

Mr. WEISS. Congressman, not only are there ideas, there are proposals. There are companies, investors, who would like to help migrate from oil and coal to alternative energy and modernize the grid. We agree, it is a dire problem. None of those investors and none of those companies are going to invest in the chaos of the current economy. It needs to be stabilized, but we do think that there is capital that can come in to solve this.

Mr. WESTERMAN. I yield back, Mr. Chairman.

The CHAIRMAN. Mr. Gallego.

Mr. GALLEGO. Thank you, Mr. Chair.

Mr. Weiss, you have mentioned about the need to have economic development as the three-step process to right the ship of Puerto Rico. So far you mentioned EITC. I have some concerns with this. I represent what you could also describe as areas that are mini-Puerto Ricos, 12 percent unemployment, businesses not moving in, things of that nature.

But EITC is very helpful for my constituents because it does bring a little more extra income into their family. And it is also great for the economy because it spurs economic growth. The problem with that is, when you have 12 percent unemployment and growing, many, many people in Puerto Rico are not going to be benefiting from EITC. In terms of spurring the economy, what it will do is spur retail work, but not necessarily any other type of economic jobs, because they still import about 85 percent of everything into that island.

One of the areas I would like to see if we could explore—in my younger years, I worked for the city of Phoenix, and we did some work in terms of economic development—is maybe looking at trying to bring the HUBZone status to the whole island. That has been very helpful for my area, in terms of bringing economic productivity, some new industries, especially light manufacturing, which could be very beneficial to Puerto Rico, as well as potentially trying to use either IDAs or New Market Tax Credits, any creative way possible to basically bring a lot more interest back to Puerto Rico.

I believe with the proper set of tools that could potentially come from this oversight committee in terms of recommendations, or us, as Members of Congress, actually passing these types of policies that would be helpful, that we could actually help spur that. Are there any other ideas besides EITC that you all are thinking about doing?

Mr. WEISS. We would be open to working with you on additional ideas.

EITC does three things in Puerto Rico. Number one, it puts money in the pockets of hard-working families. The average wage in Puerto Rico is $19,000. This would be spent. Second, it provides an incentive to join the formal workforce. There is a 40 percent labor force participation rate in Puerto Rico. And, third, we talked about long-term revenues. Over time it expands the revenue base as people join that workforce.

But we don't mean to propose this to the exclusion of other creative ideas, and we would be happy to work with your office in identifying other options.

Mr. GALLEGO. Thank you. And I yield back the remainder of my time to Congressman Gutierrez.

Mr. GUTIERREZ. Thank you so much, Congressman.

Again, Mr. Weiss, it is interesting to hear that we talk first about a control board, a control board accepted by the people in Puerto Rico. But of course, you have to accept the control board to move forward. You are still imposing a control board, because if you don't, then there is no solution to the current crisis in Puerto Rico. Again, the solution emanates without a fair distribution of power between the people of Puerto Rico and the Congress of the United States.

My point is the following. I am sorry my friend, Mr. Labrador, a fellow Puerto Rican, has suggested that it is not being bipartisan to suggest that the House of Representatives, the People's House, simply listen to the people of Puerto Rico and travel there. And to suggest that the people of Puerto Rico simply feel that this Congress is putting all of the burden, much as you have suggested, Mr. Weiss, you have never come here to talk about the merchant marine tax of billions of dollars on the people of Puerto Rico, billions of dollars, because we must use U.S. flag ships, you have not talked about that. You have not talked about the unilateral defunding of the economic tool under section 936 that the Congress of the United States—you have not spoken about the decimation of the agriculture in Puerto Rico because of policies conducted right here from Washington, DC.

All I am saying is, if the people of Puerto Rico are going to have energy and they can harness their wind, they can harness their sun, why don't we talk about those kinds of—see, then, as I have spoken to the people of Puerto Rico, they feel that there is a balance. They are saying there is a joint responsibility, but it seems to me that all of the responsibility seems to be weighed on the people of Puerto Rico. I think that that is an unfair development. Let's listen to them. Thank you so much.

Mrs. LUMMIS [presiding]. The gentleman's time has expired. The Chair recognizes Mr. Hardy.

Mr. HARDY. Thank you. Mr. Weiss, thank you for being here. You mentioned that the Puerto Rican debt payments of nearly $800 million in constitutionally prioritized debt are unlikely to be made. What impact—and I apologize if any of these questions have been asked since I was late—but what impact will that have, not only on if they fail and are prioritized over the credit markets, what will that do to not only the structure and future bonding of government GO bonds in the future to Puerto Rico, but what will it do outside of the market, over the country?

Mr. WEISS. In our judgment, those payments in July, if they are not made, will provoke chaos in the Puerto Rican municipal bond market. At the same time, I should mention there is a history of setting aside monthly amounts to build up these lump-sum payments as they come due. One of the actions that the Governor and the local legislature have taken was to stop making those setasides. So there is no assurance that that payment can be made.

And I should mention this is why we need to act now—because the consequences of a non-payment of that debt in July would be devastating for the economy of Puerto Rico. And this talk of audited financials, I would like to be clear, we do not need the audited financials to know that there is a crisis. There is a crisis.

There is plenty of information that has been released by forensic accountants. There is no doubt, even by bond investors, that there is default risk. All of the rating agencies have put these bonds at the lowest possible rating as prime for default. So yes, we need to produce audited financials. But there is a crisis, and we need to act now.

Mr. HARDY. But to add to that question, what I was trying to ask is—default happens—if it happens, does that cause concerns outside of Puerto Rico to bond shareholders for future GO bonds?

Mr. WEISS. I mentioned a report that was issued by Nuveen, one of the largest municipal bond traditional investors, just yesterday. They say very clearly that the best thing that can happen for municipal markets is for the Puerto Rican crisis to be resolved quickly, in a framework of Federal restructuring, and that the worst outcome for municipal markets is a protracted, disorderly default.

Mr. HARDY. You talked earlier about how this independent board has worked in other avenues for restructuring debt. Would you mind telling me what the make up of this board would be, overall? What individuals would be on this board?

Mr. WEISS. In our written testimony, we gave some particulars— we think that a majority of the board should be Puerto Rican residents, and that there obviously needs to be substantial expertise, not just in financial restructuring but economic expertise should be representative of stakeholders. And importantly, it should be fully independent of the political process, which is to say not elected officials, and no real or perceived conflicts of interest.

Mr. HARDY. If individuals from Puerto Rico are added to this board, does that possibly create a political challenge there? Or does this independence—will it look at it in an objective way to make sure that we always are moving forward in the right direction to solve this problem versus maybe some combative areas of it, or how does that——

Mr. WEISS. I mean——

Mr. HARDY. Any concern at all?

Mr. WEISS. Based on all of our interactions with the Puerto Rican business leaders and workers, we believe that there is a real and deep base of independent problem-solving Puerto Rican residents who would be ideally suited to this kind of responsibility.

Mr. HARDY. Thank you, and I yield back.

The CHAIRMAN [presiding]. Mr. Polis.

Mr. POLIS. Thank you, Mr. Chairman. We all know that this is the third hearing we have had regarding the Puerto Rican debt crisis. Frankly, I am disappointed we have not gotten to the point where we can have meaningful discussions about imminent action that needs to occur with regard to the financial crisis occurring every day in Puerto Rico, with over $70 billion in public debt. I think we are obligated to have an open dialogue about the use of Chapter 9 or other innovative options. We need to consider restructuring the debt in a responsible manner for any of these growth scenarios to be able to take hold.

Mr. Weiss, since this is the third hearing on the Puerto Rico debt crisis in our committee, can you speak to the urgency of taking immediate action for the people of Puerto Rico?

Mr. WEISS. Thank you for that question. The urgency could not be more apparent. When I testified before the Senate in October, I said that there could be a humanitarian crisis. I said today that I think there are already signs of humanitarian crisis. Out-migration has doubled in the last year. Again, it is 2.5 percent, as 85,000 Puerto Ricans are out-migrating today, versus 40,000 just 2 years ago. There are hospitals that have been forced to close doors.

And again, the Government Development Bank is dangerously under-capitalized. The payments which are coming in May and in July are unlikely to be made. There has already been default, there is already litigation——

Mr. POLIS. And speaking of the urgency, whatever the restructuring, the rebuilding, and the recapitalization steps that occur, do they get easier or harder if Congress continues to delay?

Mr. WEISS. There is no ability to delay.

Mr. POLIS. There is no ability to delay. Thank you.

I want to also talk about a lot of the testimony that was about ideas for growth and how we can grow the Puerto Rican economy. One of the pillars, of course, promotion of economic measures aimed at growth. But the only economic measures specifically I have heard from you relate to the EITC, which you mentioned earlier. There is also the treatment of Medicaid benefits.

I fear that those are far too mild for what we actually need to encourage economic growth in Puerto Rico. Would the Treasury consider exploring additional growth options, like using the tax code to provide incentives for new corporate investments in Puerto Rico? I would certainly be willing to work with you on those kinds of proposals. Are those the kinds of things that you would be open to?

Mr. WEISS. Yes. The necessary conditions are restructuring and oversight, but we are open to other ideas that would stimulate long-term growth.

Mr. POLIS. I thank you, and I yield the remainder of my time to Mr. Pierluisi from Puerto Rico.

Mr. PIERLUISI. Thank you. I should state for the record that I am the duly-elected representative of Puerto Rico in this Congress. And even though not everybody in Puerto Rico voted for me, when I raise my voice on the Floor of the House or at this hearing, I am speaking for the people of Puerto Rico.

So, the notion that the people of Puerto Rico are not being heard in Congress or by this committee is wrong. I do appreciate when my fellow Puerto Ricans who are actually voting Members in this Congress come to assist me, and I know that they identify themselves with my constituents. But let's not lose sight of that fact.

I vouch for the fact that Chairman Bishop has been working closely with me, and I look forward to continuing to work closely with Chairman Bishop so we come up with adequate bipartisan legislation to deal with this crisis.

Having said that, I am very concerned, Mr. Weiss, about the impending defaults either in May, or looks definitely like in July. What is Treasury doing to encourage creditors to provide necessary short-term financing, or necessary forbearance, so that Puerto Rico does not go there?

Mr. WEISS. Over a cliff?

Mr. PIERLUISI. Yes.

Mr. WEISS. We are deeply concerned with the same payments. Just last week, Secretary Lew has convened creditors in different bonds to send the message that we are determined to see a solution here. The Puerto Rican people have sacrificed, and for there to be a viable solution, there needs to be broad sacrifice across all stakeholders. It cannot just come on the back of the Puerto Rican people.

And I would say that those discussions were constructive, but there will be no substitute, for the reasons that I have articulated earlier, for a comprehensive restructuring authority across the debt.

The CHAIRMAN. Thank you.

Mr. McClintock.

Mr. MCCLINTOCK. Thank you, Mr. Chairman.

Mr. Weiss, if we rewrote the rules on Puerto Rico's sovereign debt now, what would that do to the sovereign debts of the 50 states? They borrow at much lower interest rates precisely because of the rules that are in place. Puerto Rico got lower interest rates to borrow precisely because of this assurance of stability. By rewriting the laws, you shatter that understanding of stability. And this calls into question every other sovereign debt.

I am afraid the credit markets are going to say, "Well, wait a second. If they can do that to the Puerto Rican debt, they can do that for California, Illinois, and New York," and markets will respond to that by assessing this additional risk and increasing interest costs to reflect that risk. That could sink a state like California, for example, that is carrying enormous debt right now.

In fact, the governors of Alabama, Arizona, Maine, New Mexico, Nebraska, and North Dakota wrote a letter to this effect just this past month. They said, "Of most concern to us as governors, granting Puerto Rico such unprecedented bankruptcy authority would likely raise the borrowing costs of our states, reducing our ability to invest in vital services and eroding investor confidence in the whole notion of full faith and credit debt."

Indeed, the National Governors Association has already warned against this in 2011, noting that states should not be given the right to declare bankruptcy themselves because the result in market volatility would raise the cost of state governments precipitously.

Now, I realize we are not talking about Chapter 9 bankruptcy, per se, but the same principle applies to rewriting the rules after they have been agreed to and loans have been made under those rules. What is your response to that?

Mr. WEISS. Respectfully, Congressman, we do not share that analysis. As Treasury, we have given this substantial thought.

First, Puerto Rico, to state the obvious, is not——

Mr. MCCLINTOCK. But if you do not share that concern that has been expressed by many other governors, it is being expressed universally throughout the credit markets, that is a reflection on the bad advice and thinking that is going on in Treasury right now, and that is even a bigger concern.

Mr. WEISS. Again, traditional municipal bond investors—Nuveen, Blackrock, agencies such as Moody's—nearly universally say that the healthiest thing that could happen for municipal bond investors would be for there to be a federally legislated restructuring——

Mr. MCCLINTOCK. With all due respect, that is precisely the opposite of what the investors are saying, and they are the ones that will be charging the interest costs to every other state in the country.

As a result of this action that you are proposing, I am concerned that we are going to see a rapid escalation of borrowing costs for the states that right now enjoy the understanding that there is a stability to the rules under which they are making these loans.

Mr. WEISS. Congressman, there are material differences between Puerto Rico, states, and municipalities. First, it is completely cordoned off by investors. There have been no traditional municipal bond new issuances——

Mr. MCCLINTOCK. But the principle remains and the principle adheres to the sovereign debts of every one of the 50 states, which you would be directly undermining by this reckless——

Mr. WEISS. We face——

Mr. MCCLINTOCK [continuing]. Policy. Let me go on. Puerto Rico seems to me to be a poster child for a heavily regulated and government-managed economy and Keynesian deficit stimulus spending. It has a bloated government workforce, and all of these policies have been a complete and unmitigated disaster for the economy of Puerto Rico. It seems to me the economy does not need more regulation in government management, it needs less.

It seems to me that this is an opportunity to make Puerto Rico an enterprise zone, to dramatically reduce the tax and regulatory burdens, and turn Puerto Rico into a Hong Kong of the Caribbean. That means providing relief from the Federal corporate tax rates, getting rid of the capital gains taxes on investment in Puerto Rico, a FICA holiday, energy de-regulation, obviously exemption from the Jones Act to spur maritime commerce, and relief from the minimum wage to spur hiring.

Puerto Rico is a cruise ship destination, for heaven's sake. It is one of the most beautiful parts of the world. They have the most fertile soil and climate imaginable. They have access to Atlantic shipping and trade. The only thing they lack is wise public policy. If we were to make these changes, wouldn't we be likely to see rapid recapitalization of the economy, as corporations around the world assess these changes and realize they can enjoy both a free market and live in an island paradise?

Mr. WEISS. Congressman, what are we to do when the $2 billion of debt comes due on July 1?

Mr. MCCLINTOCK. Administer them as the current rules provide.

The CHAIRMAN. I am sorry, everyone owes me 5 seconds now.

Mr. Serrano, our rules say we have to have the committee first, but I am going to let you go before I do. But let me finish the rest of this committee first, if possible.

Mr. Gohmert.

Mr. GOHMERT. Thank you, Mr. Chairman. And thank you, Counselor, for being here. Have you ever done manual labor, like with a shovel, digging?

Mr. WEISS. Yes.

Mr. GOHMERT. Oh, good. You had me worried there, because of the long pause.

Mr. WEISS. Oh, I actually did not hear the example you gave.

Mr. GOHMERT. Oh, OK, yes. Just have you ever used a shovel and dug a hole.

Mr. WEISS. A lot.

Mr. GOHMERT. So I would take it, then, you have filled one in before.

Mr. WEISS. Yes.

Mr. GOHMERT. Yes.

Mr. WEISS. With my sons, yes.

Mr. GOHMERT. Yes. And that makes it interesting with your sons. Because it seems like what we have seen in Puerto Rico, they have dug themselves a hole and, as has been fully discussed here today, they are needing help getting out of the hole.

But I also recall my friend, Luis Fortuno, trying to get Puerto Rico on the right track. And my recollection of events, he laid off thousands of government workers, trying to get on track.

Mr. WEISS. Tens of thousands.

Mr. GOHMERT. Tens of thousands. Yes, around 30,000, was that right?

Mr. WEISS. I think so.

Mr. GOHMERT. Yes, and thinking that if we can show the total United States, show the world investors we can get our debt under control, we can stop digging a hole, then we have a chance to get on track and the money will be well invested here in Puerto Rico. Obviously, he lost the next election because they did not want a governor who was laying off that many government workers.

I pulled up—this says it is copyright 2016—but a list of cities in Puerto Rico by population and by percent of government employees. Apparently, Culebra, 1,868 population, percent government employees, 45.28; then—sorry if I butcher the name—Utuado, Puerto Rico, 35,015 and 40.06 percent of their population is government workers; and next, 27,913 population, 39.07 percent is government workers.

It seems like if we set up some kind of plan—and there are indications they are going to need Federal money, Federal help—we would be taking a shovel and trying to fill the hole back in. The trouble seems to be, with the high percentage of government workers in Puerto Rico, that they are going to be digging the hole at the same time we are trying to fill it in. I do not see how that would encourage capital to come rushing in, especially when they see the example that people are not going to get a dollar for a dollar that was invested in the original bonds.

So, I know you are Counselor to the Secretary of the Treasury. I looked that up during the long time we were waiting. It is a person trained to give guidance. I would take it you give the Secretary of the Treasury guidance, correct?

Mr. WEISS. Yes, sir.

Mr. GOHMERT. What kind of guidance do you give the Secretary of the Treasury on helping a gorgeous place like Puerto Rico, who continues to dig the hole while you are wanting to give advice on filling the hole? I mean do you tell him that they are continuing to dig the hole, the percentage of government workers is still going to be just a powerful suck on the amount of capital there is in the country?

Mr. WEISS. Congressman, this is an enormously difficult problem, but it is also a great opportunity. And what I have said, and what the Administration believes, is this is one of those rare chances where we, working with Congress, can actually solve something, which no governor of the last five has been able to do on their own.

If we restructure the debt under appropriate oversight with real fiscal planning, real budgeting, and performance in line with budgets, that is what is going to get stability back on the island.

Mr. GOHMERT. And then that is going to send a message to the people of the island, "We can keep electing governors who will not get the percentage of employees to the government under control, so we can keep digging while they are filling it in." That is my concern. Thank you, I yield back.

The CHAIRMAN. Thank you. I know we told you we would be here until noon, but if you give me another 15 minutes we can get everything done.

Mr. WEISS. Yes, sir.

The CHAIRMAN. Mrs. Lummis.

Mrs. LUMMIS. Well, I want to thank you for your ideas on oversight and orderly restructuring. I believe in the short term that is an essential component to moving forward. If we could sort of marry the short-term idea of oversight and orderly restructuring with some of the other longer term ideas that were expressed by members of this committee, I think that Puerto Rico will not only survive this, but thrive this. Thank you very much for working with our committee.

Mr. Chairman, thank you for holding this hearing. I yield back the balance of my time.

Mr. WEISS. Thank you, Congresswoman.

The CHAIRMAN. Mr. Serrano, before I ask my questions, let me yield to you so you have a chance to talk to the witness.

Mr. SERRANO. Thank you, Mr. Chairman. I also want to join you and the other Members in thanking you for holding the hearing, and for giving me an opportunity, as a non-member of this committee, to participate.

Mr. Weiss, I believe that you are a friend of Puerto Rico, and I believe that you want to solve the issue. But we keep making a mistake in this Congress and the Administration, and it does not matter what party is in power, we make the mistake. Whenever we speak of status, we make it sound like status is not the issue, that the time is not right to discuss status. I would argue that status is the problem, and it is always the right time to discuss status.

You, yourself, when asked about status, you kind of glossed over it, and I say this with all due respect and admiration. You said, "The people of Puerto Rico," I think you said, "have to resolve this. We agree that it has to be done."

First of all, that is a mistake. The people of Puerto Rico did not invade the United States. The United States invaded the people of Puerto Rico. At the minimum, the U.S. Congress has to tell Puerto Rico what is available on the table for a change in status. It is obvious that the present status is a problem. Why is it a problem?

If there has ever been a need for proof that Puerto Rico is a colony, we just found it. Puerto Rico cannot restructure its debt without permission from the United States. Puerto Rico cannot apply Chapter 9 without being included again. I have heard people who believe in Puerto Rico sovereignty, and even Puerto Rico independence, total independence, say, "We don't have the tools." Those tools are acquired through statehood, independence, or free association.

My question to you is—well, not this part, because this part is my comment. I think that what we are doing now is putting a Band-Aid on a major issue, because 2 years from now, 5 years from now, 10 years from now, the issue will be back again because Puerto Rico does not have the ability to resolve.

I read recently or heard recently, just to give you an example of where Puerto Rico finds itself, Mr. Chairman—I may be wrong, so I will stand corrected ahead of time, but I heard that Puerto Rico was going to buy plantains from the Dominican Republic and was told by the Federal Government it could not do so without its approval. That is how bad it has gotten at times.

I remember once Puerto Rico was going to have a foreign country irrigate some lands, and they were told by the State Department, "You cannot ask that foreign country to irrigate any land." So you know what Puerto Rico is? It is not treated equally. Only in war time is it treated equally.

So, my question to you is—you will be consulted as this bill is put together. You will be more than consulted, not you, but the Treasury Department and you, probably, one of the leaders in it. Would the Treasury Department consider making sure that that bill has language that says, "But we cannot ignore the fact that the status issue has to be resolved, and resolved once and for all"? Or are we going to continue to say that it is up to the people of Puerto Rico, the recipients of colonialism, that have to undo colonialism?

Because I can tell you, as a member of the Appropriations Committee, and I was born in the colony and now oversee the colony, so I probably need a psychiatrist on colonialism to deal with my situation, but I can tell you, as a member of the Appropriations Committee, that all the states get what applies to them, and then whatever is left over—even to get Puerto Rico on the back of a quarter during that program where we had states on the back of a quarter, I had to include special legislation to get Puerto Rico on the back of a quarter. Not a big deal, but it makes the point.

So, my question to you is, can we have the Treasury Department suggest strong language that says, "But don't forget, you have to resolve the status question"?

Mr. WEISS. Congressman, thank you for your compliments at your opening. I would like to return them. I have learned an enormous amount in our interactions with you.

Status is vitally important. Where I would like to disagree, respectfully, this is not a Band-Aid. This is a life-saving procedure that we are discussing. If we do not restructure this debt, if we are faced with the events that Congressman Pierluisi described in May and July, Puerto Rico's very survival is at stake. We don't think about this as a Band-Aid, we think about it as an absolutely necessary action.

Mr. SERRANO. Reclaiming my 5 seconds, it is a Band-Aid in my opinion, because we will resolve it for today, but we will not resolve it for 5 years from now, and that has to be dealt with at some time. Thank you, Mr. Chairman.

The CHAIRMAN. Thank you.

Mr. Lamborn. Better late than never.

Mr. LAMBORN. Thank you, Mr. Chairman, for having this hearing. Mr. Weiss, thank you for being here. I apologize I was not here earlier, I was in a mark-up in another committee. But I just wanted to get a little bit of background, take advantage of the work you have done in working on a plan.

Let me ask a little bit about prioritization. If you had your way in the plan that the Treasury Department is working on, how specifically—for instance, would government workers with pensions be treated under the plan that you are proposing?

Mr. WEISS. We believe that all of the debt needs to be part of the discussion, but that we would be open to respecting existing priorities and claims within that.

As to pensions, it was incorrectly reported this morning that we thought that should be prioritized above everything. But I do need to say these pensions are completely unfunded, and we are deeply concerned that they be protected. There is about a 2 percent funding ratio on a pension that supports 330,000 Americans working for the public municipalities and government in Puerto Rico. That is a completely unheard-of funding ratio. And these are not gold-plated pensions. The average monthly payment is around $1,200, sometimes less.

So, yes, we believe pensions need to be protected, but we would like to work together with you, and we really have had good bipartisan discussions with the Chairman and his staff about how to put all of the pieces of this together such that there is the most fair and equitable treatment we can design for all stakeholders.

Mr. LAMBORN. OK, thank you. Let me ask about the energy angle on this, and PREPA, and the electrical generation. What are some of your thoughts or recommendations on that debt, which is about, I think, 11 or 12 percent of the total debt?

Mr. WEISS. Yes, the PREPA debt is around 11 or 12 percent of the total debt. There is a voluntary agreement that is in place that has been worked on for about a year-and-a-half. It has, I believe, 70 percent creditor approval. And it would be helped by orderly restructuring, because they could then go on and finalize it. They would not face the problem of having to deal with the remaining 30 percent who are holding out, hoping for a better deal, or hoping for some other outcome.

So, we think our restructuring authority could be used to help solve PREPA, and we discussed earlier that we do think that the energy grid and the energy generation sources in Puerto Rico badly need to be modernized, upgraded, and diversified away from oil, gas, and coal. But we also are optimistic on that score. We think, if we pursue this plan and stabilize the economy, that there will be ample third-party capital and third-party industry that will be interested in investing in those areas.

Mr. LAMBORN. In order to modernize and to do it quickly, I think you would agree with me time is of the essence. Would we want to have some kind of ability to cut through red tape that would currently maybe make a project that could—you know, a construction project that would take 1 or 2 years, when you add all the layers of regulatory reviews, may take 5 or 10 years. Would you agree with me that we can do better in cutting through red tape?

Mr. WEISS. You know, we have heard the same, anecdotally, complaints from investors in respect of the permitting and bureaucratic process. But the real problem that investors face today is like in any case: nobody is going to put money to work in an economy that is in free fall and in full-blown financial crisis.

We need to stem this crisis. Once we stem the crisis, there is capital. There are people of good will who want to invest in Puerto Rico, and there is a future for the people of Puerto Rico. There are going to be new jobs. There will be new investment. And it is ultimately our hope that all of those who have out-migrated will see that opportunity and will begin to return.

Mr. LAMBORN. OK. I look forward to working with you and the Chairman and every interested party, trying to make this work as efficiently as possible and in an expedited way. I can think of examples of red tape that we might want to look at as part of this whole process.

Mr. Chairman, thanks for having this hearing, and I yield back.

The CHAIRMAN. Thank you.

Mr. Weiss, let me ask the last questions here. I like going last, because there are basically very few people around to hear me.

So, in an effort simply to capture what the breadth of this situation is, let me quickly summarize. Puerto Rico has about $70 billion in debt from bonds. The pension liability is $46 billion, they have $2 billion in assets to cover it. They do not have access to credit markets or to borrow money. There is significant out-migration, as you have mentioned. The Government Development Bank, where many of their deposits are held, is in peril. The Governor has authorized a billion dollars in some unsustainable liquidity actions, including withholding tax refunds; selling assets from pension funds; taking money dedicated to one group of creditors to pay others; and the fact is there could easily be a central government that would be forced to shut down.

With that background, and based on Treasury's analysis of the situation, should there be any sacred cows that are put on the table? Is anything so sacrosanct that it cannot be discussed by any kind of oversight board or institution in seeking a solution?

Mr. WEISS. We believe that we all must be prepared to question our basic tenets. We appreciate the bipartisan spirit of the discussion that we have had with you and your staff. We would not want to compromise the self-governance of Puerto Rico in the process. We would not want to put at risk the payments that are due to pensioners.

The CHAIRMAN. OK, we have that down well, yes.

45

Mr. WEISS. But fundamentally, we think this has required enormous sacrifice on the part of the people of Puerto Rico, and that all of us who are part of this solution should work in an openminded way in order to construct something. Time is the chief enemy of this crisis.

The CHAIRMAN. In regard to the bonds that are outstanding, does Treasury have any estimate as to how many of those bonds are actually held by pensioners in the United States?

Mr. WEISS. There are not precise estimates of this. We think that a substantial portion are held through a couple of mutual funds who have stayed substantially invested in Puerto Rico. Most mutual funds, when non-investment grade happened 2½ years ago, sold out. We think that there are about 30–35 percent of the bonds there held by hedge funds.

The CHAIRMAN. You noted in your testimony, as well, that Puerto Rico's debt is unusually complex. In your experience, how would you rate that complexity with debts to other situations in which you have encountered.

Mr. WEISS. Very creative.

The CHAIRMAN. Well then, we will be creative when we come up with something here.

In a previous hearing, Mayor Williams was asked how a strong oversight board could respect Puerto Rico's self-government. We have touched on that with many Members here today. In essence, his answer was the oversight board needed to hire good people who will work with the Commonwealth's government and its affiliates to promote the trust that is required for a good working relationship. Do you agree with that assessment?

Mr. WEISS. We believe that there are people of good will across Puerto Rico and across the United States in general who would feel a mission in solving this crisis that is of such historic magnitude. We think that there is an ample talent pool, both on the island and across the mainland, of people who would feel extraordinarily motivated. Because again, this is not just a crisis, it is an amazing opportunity. It is one of those rare cases where we, collectively, can put an end to this crisis. That is a calling that we think that many would respond to.

The CHAIRMAN. Thank you. I appreciate that. Let me ask one last question, if I can get it in here.

Based on Treasury's analysis, is it clear how the debt would be classified? Like, Commonwealth debt versus public corporation debt.

Mr. WEISS. Yes, we think that there is about $50 billion of debt that is supported by the taxing authority of the Commonwealth, that there is a little under $20 billion that is either public corporation, like PREPA and the municipalities. And it is that $50 billion where there is the biggest problem, because it is the $50 billion that is paid out of the general fund.

So, all of the debt needs to be restructured within the $50 billion. There are revenue bonds, there are general obligation bonds. We would be happy to send you our schedule of what we think is outstanding.

The CHAIRMAN. All right. I appreciate that. Mr. Weiss, I appreciate you being here, for your patience with us, answering all the questions that have been thrown at you. It is also very difficult, I realize, because you are the only person on the panel. Usually you have a chance to take a breather and let somebody else answer a question, eventually. But you did it all.

Mr. WEISS. May I exceed by 10 seconds to thank you, this committee, and your staff? I opened on a note of optimism. I hope I may close on a note of optimism. We think there is broad recognition of this crisis today, and we do think there are very positive discussions taking place. We may have disagreements amongst us, but there is a sense of urgency. If there is a will, there is a way.

The CHAIRMAN. If you are going to thank us, I will give you another 10.

[Laughter.]

The CHAIRMAN. That is OK, we got it. There are a couple of documents that were presented that need a unanimous consent to be added to the record. We have the documents here.

[No response.]

The CHAIRMAN. If there is no objection, great.

We do have a Committee Rule 4(h) that is—yes, 4(h), cute name—that says that the Committee Record is going to be held open for at least 10 business days. If other Members have questions, we may be asking you to respond to those questions that are submitted in writing.

If there is no further business, with my appreciation to the witness, appreciation to the committee members, as well as our guests for being here, we thank you. This committee stands adjourned.

[Whereupon, at 12:20 p.m., the committee was adjourned.]

[ADDITIONAL MATERIALS SUBMITTED FOR THE RECORD]

PREPARED STATEMENT OF THE HON. GREGORIO KILILI CAMACHO SABLAN, A DELEGATE FROM THE NORTHERN MARIANA ISLANDS

Mr. Chairman, thank you for the opportunity to add a few comments to the record of today's hearing on "The U.S. Department of the Treasury's Analysis of the Situation in Puerto Rico."

I understand our focus is on Puerto Rico, because that part of our Nation is defaulting on its debt, something that has not occurred in my district, the Northern Mariana Islands, or other U.S. insular areas.

But it could. Just this week the Marianas government on court order had to scrape together $1.8 million to pay its retirees after cutting their bi-monthly pensions by 25 percent earlier in the month. But there remains an unfunded pension liability in the hundreds of millions of dollars.

What is happening now in Puerto Rico should be a warning of what could happen in other U.S. insular areas. And it would be wise policy and an exercise in foresight to address root causes of the fiscal problems in all the islands, when we address the problem in Puerto Rico.

In fact, the Treasury Department and the Administration have already put one idea on the table that would help with solvency in all the insular areas. This is to bring the islands closer to the national Medicaid program in which the Federal Government pays more of state health care costs, depending on the proportion of low-income persons in that state.

The islands bear a disproportionate share of those Medicaid costs. And this burden contributes to fiscal stress and reduces the quality of health care in the insular areas.

Treasury proposed in its Puerto Rico roadmap last fall that Congress remove the cap on Medicaid and increase the Federal Medicaid match for Puerto Rico. And the President confirmed in his budget submission this month that it is intended that this Medicaid reform apply to all the U.S. insular areas.

I support that proposal.

But there is one other policy reform that would improve the fiscal situation in all the islands that—inexplicably—the Administration has confined to Puerto Rico. This is extension of the Earned Income Tax Credit.

There is broad agreement on both sides of the aisle that the EITC is a policy that supports economic growth and, thus, improves the fiscal health of a community. Speaker Ryan is a fan, because the EITC, unlike conventional welfare programs, rewards work. It encourages those who are unemployed to get a job, support themselves and their families, become contributing members of society.

And the Administration has proposed—both in the Treasury roadmap and in the President's budget for fiscal 2017—using the EITC to bring people into the workforce in Puerto Rico. But not in any of the other insular areas.

This week at the annual meeting of the Interagency Group on Insular Affairs, the Administration explained that extending the Earned Income Tax Credit to the Northern Marianas, American Samoa, Guam, and the Virgin Islands was not necessary, because those areas "are not in dire straits."

I ask you, do we have to see an insular area in fiscal collapse before we take action? Or do we help avoid the kind of problem we now have in Puerto Rico by taking action to treat U.S. citizens living in all the insular areas more like they would be treated if they lived in any U.S. state?

My fellow Delegates from American Samoa, and Guam are co-sponsors of my legislation, H.R. 4309, that would provide Federal support for the Earned Income Tax Credit in our jurisdictions. And I strongly recommend that this committee assure that in any legislation, addressing the fiscal crisis in Puerto Rico and including reform of the Medicaid program and extension of EITC to Puerto Rico, all of the U.S. insular areas we represent be equally included.

Thank you.

————

Carlos A. Colon-De-Armas, Ph.D.
Professor of Finance, Graduate School of Business, University of Puerto Rico

**Answers to the Questions for the Record
Submitted by Senator Orrin G. Hatch
U.S. Senate Committee on the Judiciary**

**Hearing on Puerto Rico's Fiscal Problems: Examining the Source and Exploring the Solution
December 1, 2015, Washington, DC**

The three questions submitted revolve around the issue of extending to the Government of Puerto Rico access to bankruptcy proceedings. Therefore, it seems important to preface my answers by expressing my two main objections to the use of bankruptcy as the way to solve the fiscal problems faced by the Government of the Island: (1) it would worsen the economic situation in Puerto Rico, and (2) it is not supported by the available evidence.

In my written testimony, and in the Q&A portion of the hearing, I addressed the impact of bankruptcy to the economy. In essence, I explained that the fiscal crisis was not caused by a weakening economy, but rather, that it was the government, in the way it handled its finances, that damaged the economy. It did so by using its limited borrowing capacity, that was supposed to be utilized only to finance public investments, and used it instead to finance spending. As a result, an already fragile economy experienced a significant loss of investments and deteriorated even more. To revert this trend, and to fix the economic crisis, public and private investments on the Island must be increased and the business climate in Puerto Rico should be improved. For these investments to take place, financing is necessary. for which access to financial markets is essential. Bankruptcy, however, would close access to financial markets for Puerto Rico for an indeterminate number of years, to the detriment of the quality of life of the residents of the Island.

Regarding the reason to seek bankruptcy, it is important to understand the debt burden calculation that serves as the basis for that option. To start, consider the consolidated budget for the entire Government of Puerto Rico, for fiscal year 2016, which totals $28,808 million. Within that budget, the aggregate debt service for the entire public debt of Puerto Rico, including General Obligations, COFINA, all public corporations, and all other debts, amounts to $4,491 million. That debt service payment represents 16% of the entire consolidated budget. Nevertheless, on page 17 of The Puerto Rico Fiscal and Economic Growth Plan, prepared by the Working Group

48

for the Fiscal and Economic Recovery of Puerto Rico pursuant to Puerto Rico Executive Order 2015–022, dated September 9, 2015, the debt service as a percent of revenues for fiscal year 2016 is calculated to be 42%. On that same page, they make the same calculations for the projected figures for fiscal years 2017 through 2020 and the result amounts to approximately 40% for the five years presented. That 40% figure is cited by many people as the public debt burden of the Government of Puerto Rico, and it is used as the justification for seeking the right to declare bankruptcy. On closer examination, it is easy to see that the calculation of a 40% debt burden is wrong. To see why, let's examine the detailed calculations for fiscal year 2016 presented in the following table.

Puerto Rico Public Debt Burden for Fiscal Year 2016:
Working Group vs. Consolidated Budget

	Working Group	Consolidated Budget
Revenues		
General Fund and other select revenues (1)	$8,503	$8,503
GDB net operating revenues (1)	(96)	(96)
COFINA (1)	696	696
HTA revenues (1)	677	677
Increased sales tax and VAT (2)		1,121
Other revenues (plug)		10,535
Federal transfers (1)		6,477
Loans and bond issues (2)		895
Total revenues	$9,780	$28,808
Debt service		
GOs and selected agencies (1)	$4,130	$4,130
Other debt service (plug)		361
Total debt service	$4,130	$4,491
Debt service as a percent of total revenues	42%	16%

(1) From page 17 of The Puerto Rico Fiscal and Economic Growth Plan ("FEGP") prepared by the Working Group for the Fiscal and Economic Recovery of Puerto Rico pursuant to Puerto Rico Executive Order 2015–022, dated September 9, 2015.

(2) Available at: http://www2.pr.gov/presupuestos/presupuestoaprobado2015-2016/Pages/default.aspx.

As can be seen from the table, to make its calculations, the Working Group uses only $9,780 of revenues, which represent only 34% of the consolidated budget, but includes $4,130 for debt service, which represents 92% of the entire aggregate debt service required for the year. When you include the rest of the resources available in the budget, even when you add the rest of the debt service, the proper debt service as a percent of the total budget is significantly lower, at 16%.

The Working Group performed its calculation using as its basis the report by Krueger, Anne O., Ranjit Teja, and Andrew Wolfe, *Puerto Rico—A Way Forward*, June 29, 2015 (updated on July 13, 2015), the so called "Krueger Report". Accordingly, the argument is that "the General Fund alone . . . does not adequately capture the total financing needs of the Commonwealth." (See the FEGP, p. 15.)

Although it may be true that the General Fund represents only a portion of the Government of Puerto Rico, and although certain items in the consolidated budget (e.g., federal funds, loans and bond issues) are not available to pay debt service, the entire consolidated budget represents the total amount of resources available to the Government of Puerto Rico to pay debt service and to provide services to the people. Therefore, if we accept the premise of the Governor of Puerto Rico, that in this fiscal crisis the debt payments must be balanced against the need to provide services to the people of the Island, the entire consolidated budget should be the basis of the analysis. After all, the funds that are not available to pay debt service may be used to provide services to the citizens. The usage of these funds for these purposes, therefore, would liberate resources that then could be used to pay debt service. Accordingly, the needs of the people and the commitments to honor debt obligations, would be effectively balanced.

It must be noted that the Krueger Report "was prepared at the request of legal counsel." (See the Krueger Report, p. 2.) As such, it may well serve as the basis for a particular legal strategy like, for example, bankruptcy. It is doubtful, however, that it should serve as the basis upon which to base a sound public policy.

Based on the above, the proper debt service burden of the Government of Puerto Rico, when correctly calculated, is 16%,[1] and not 40%. In that regard, it is worth mentioning that in a report by Moody's Analytics (Zandi, Mark, Dan White, and Bernard Yaros, *Puerto Rico Looks Into the Abyss*, November 2015), that unquestioningly accepts the 40% debt service figure calculated by the Working Group, the authors argue that a debt service burden of 20% of government revenues is "sustainable" (p. 1). By the same logic, if 20% is sustainable, a 16% debt burden does not justify the use of bankruptcy.

In summary, the use of bankruptcy is not justified by the available evidence.

I now proceed to answer each of the questions specifically.

Question #1: Would extending Chapter 9 to Puerto Rico carry any negative consequences for the island? I'm not talking just about bondholders. I'm talking about the commonwealth as an entity. If Congress extended Chapter 9 to Puerto Rico and island municipalities began taking advantage of Chapter 9, how would that impact the island's bond rating, its creditworthiness, its attractiveness as an investment location, etc.? Is there a scenario under which extending Chapter 9 to Puerto Rico would actually make the island's fiscal situation worse?

Answer to Question #1: First, it is important to make the distinction between having access to bankruptcy proceedings and actually using it. That distinction is relevant because every state of the Union has access to bankruptcy protection for their public corporations and that access does not seem to have affected their credit quality.

As I indicated in the introduction, if the Government of Puerto Rico were to use bankruptcy as the way to solve its fiscal crisis that would worsen the economic situation of the Island because it would close access to financial markets for an indefinite number of years which would make it impossible to undertake necessary investments on the Island. That outcome would come about, at least, for three reasons:

1. The use of bankruptcy is not justified and to argue otherwise the government and its consultants had to resort to data manipulation, as I demonstrated in the introduction.
2. Reneging on its debt commitments would constitute a drastic change in the financial tradition of the Government of Puerto Rico that, until now, had an unblemished record of meeting its debt commitments.
3. Using bankruptcy protection would constitute a change of the rules under which bonds were issued. This change of rules not only could constitute a violation of constitutional provisions that protect contractual relations, but it also would erode the confidence on the Island of potential investors.

That situation would be even worse under the proposal by the Department of Treasury that would allow the Government of Puerto Rico to seek bankruptcy protection even for debt guaranteed by the Island's Constitution.

Naturally, any situation that weakens the economy of Puerto Rico would make the fiscal situation even worse.

Question #2: We've heard arguments that extending Chapter 9 to Puerto Rico would be unfair to bondholders because it would reduce their return on their investments. Some have argued that any Chapter 9 extension should apply only to future debts. As an initial matter, it would be helpful to know whether past bankruptcy code reforms have applied to existing debts, or whether bankruptcy reforms have typically applied only to future debts. Can you offer any insight on this matter? And

[1] In my written testimony at the hearing I indicated that the debt service represents 16.8% of the consolidated budget of the Government of Puerto Rico. That calculation was based on the proposed budget. Based on the budget that was finally approved, the debt service is 16%, like it was indicated above.

if past reforms have applied to existing debts, have any of those reforms been analogous to what we're considering here—namely, extension of bankruptcy access to entities who previously had no such access? I asked this question at the hearing, but I didn't get a complete answer and I believe it's extremely important.

Answer to Question #2: I am aware of the constitutional impediments, both locally and at the federal level, to enact laws that may affect contractual relationships. At the same time, I am also cognizant of the fact that those very same Constitutions protect the power of Congress, at the federal level, and of state legislatures, at the local level, to approve laws. Balancing those two constitutional provisions is not an easy task and may require court intervention. Given that my area of expertise is not the law, on this question, I defer to those who do have that expertise.

From an economic standpoint, however, even if it were legally permissible, granting Puerto Rico access to bankruptcy protection for its existing debts is both troublesome and extremely dangerous. Utilizing bankruptcy when the debt service burden is 16% is equivalent to saying that "we can pay our debts, but we rather not pay them." Any jurisdiction acting that way, and one that does it with the express approval of Congress (via the contemporaneous extension of Chapter 9), will find it incredibly difficult to access the markets thereafter, since they are, plain and simply, refusing to pay their debts. In fact, it seems fair to say that an act of Congress that would allow a jurisdiction to avoid paying debts that it can otherwise pay would not only be unique, but it also would have disastrous consequences.

Question #3: Another question on Chapter 9 and retroactivity: If Congress steps in and changes the rules of the game after the fact to allow municipalities to discharge existing debts, do we need to worry about the message that sends to other debtors and other creditors across the country? Parties negotiate contracts according to existing laws. If we step in and suddenly change the rules, does that tell parties in other situations that the rules are actually more up for grabs than they might think? Does that tell other states or other municipalities outside Puerto Rico that if things get bad enough, Congress will simply change the rules to help ease the pressure?

Answer to Question #3: To ascertain whether granting Puerto Rico access to bankruptcy proceedings would constitute a change in the rules under which bonds were sold, I examined the official statements issued by the government of the Island as part of prior bond offerings. I did not find a direct reference to the issue of bankruptcy until the official statement issued in March 11, 2014, in which case the following disclosure was included:

> The Commonwealth is not currently eligible to seek relief under Chapter 9 of the United States Bankruptcy Code. In the future, however, new legislation could be enacted by the U.S. Congress or by the Legislative Assembly that would entitle the Commonwealth to seek the protection of a statute providing for restructuring, moratorium and similar laws affecting creditors' rights. This could affect the rights and remedies of the holders of general obligation bonds and notes of the Commonwealth, including the Bonds, and the enforceability of the Commonwealth's obligation to make payments on such general obligation bonds and notes. (Commonwealth of Puerto Rico, Official Statement issued in relation with the issuance of the $3,500,000,000 General Obligation Bonds of 2014, Series A, March 11, 2014, page 9.)

This disclosure constitutes an admission by the Government of Puerto Rico that if it were granted bankruptcy protection the rules under which bonds were issued would change. Otherwise, they would not have felt obligated to make the aforementioned disclosure.

Since it would constitute a change of rules, that would be another reason not to advocate bankruptcy as the tool to use to solve Puerto Rico's fiscal crisis. Thus, the only way in which Puerto Rico should be given access to bankruptcy protection is through a process in which that protection, instead of the primary objective, would be incidental to another decision as would be, for example, as a result of a change in the political status of Puerto Rico. Even under those conditions, however, for the reasons indicated before, I would not advocate for the Island to use that mechanism.

POSITION PAPER

Submitted by Carlos E. Chardon, Former Executive Director of the Republican Party, San Juan, Puerto Rico

Is Puerto Rico a Failing State?

Introduction

Puerto Rico has most of the characteristics of a failing state, yet its government, is still performing most of its responsibilities but for paying what it owes (bonds, suppliers, commitments to retirement funds and some operational expenditures). Non-payment of bond holders produced a crisis in 2015 which resulted in three Senate Hearings and extended into the House with two Hearings in February 2016. Those that depend on their retirement income and those that provided services (not only construction but services such as therapy for handicapped children) do not have the presence (votes) in Congress, so they are of no account. They are collateral damage.

The extent of its crisis will be gauged once the 2013–2014 certified audit (CAEP) is known and projections from thence on are known. Thus the viability of a state is a question of degree and of more or less adequately discharging the responsibilities of governance, but more importantly on who is affected by non-performance.

Its fiscal crisis is clear although not fully quantified before the CAEP is made public and, then, accounting artistry will shield the period since the certified audit. There is no reason why government practices should change overnight unless a third party becomes the arbiter of truth. This might be a function of a financial board impressed by Congress on Puerto Rico. If this were its only responsibility it would allow the population to learn what has been done with its tax money and could even identify sources for payment of debts, but would not solve the greater issue of profligate spending. It would not solve minor but important issues to a significant part of the population: who gets paid first, retirees with whom government made a commitment before the bonds were issued and the bond holders. It would not solve the possibility of a balance between woefully low pensions with no Social Security payments to supplement them (significantly below the poverty level) and pensions three and four times the average income of the population.

The nation is likely to face the issue of pensions in states and jurisdictions important electorally for coming elections and its cost could be extremely high; but they have Senators and Representatives in Congress; the elderly in the U.S. vote in disproportionately high numbers, so it is quite likely that the treatment of pensioners who vote in national elections be different from those that do not have a vote as is the case of Puerto Rico.

Puerto Rico has been compared to Greece and Argentina, and to Detroit, Washington, D.C. and New York City. Nevertheless, none of these entities had a relationship with another country similar or parallel to Puerto Rico's with the United States. Even in the case of Greece that is beholden to the European financial system, it is still a sovereign country, something that in the case of Puerto Rico is up for a decision by the U.S. Supreme Court. It's telling that whatever the outcome, the decision will be made by the U.S., not Puerto Rico.

Puerto Rico is inside the U.S. for most government issues and outside for commercial and income tax issues. The decision was not Puerto Rico's but again the U.S. Supreme Court enacting a relationship left undefined by Congress in some of its crucial aspects. These decisions are known as the Insular Cases. Even if Islanders on approving the Constitution written in 1952 through a referendum exerted some kind of sovereignty, it was not the result of Islanders making the claim or wresting the power from the U.S. government; the territorial Constitution was possible only because of an act of Congress and the end result was approved by Congress.

If Puerto Rico must be compared with another jurisdiction this might be Canada's Newfoundland in the 1930s. Newfoundland was a separate colony from Canada that was given autonomy by the British Crown. Newfoundlanders used that autonomy to destroy its finances and economy through profligate spending by its elected officials, much as was done in Puerto Rico. A British commission (perhaps the Congressionally appointed finance board) brought it back within the fold of governments responsible for its finances.

So much for the simile, for the British Royal Commission also sacked the profligate administrators, thrashed the autonomy, and forces political parties into a route for the reconstruction of the colony. Congress is unlikely to treat into these issues. The end result of the Commission was to set Newfoundland on the road to statehood within Canada (becoming a province)—again something Congress will not do given the extent of nativism and the support of discourses in the Presidential campaign of 2016 tied in the past to racism.

Still, in the chiaroscuro of governmental relations it might be argued that the parallelism of the condition of Newfoundland that led to intervention with that of Puerto Rico is astounding, although the ultimate result—integration of Newfoundland as province of Canada—is no where in an alternative. For practical matters, if it were so, the rejection of the finance board by a substantial portion of the population would be significant. It would be the equivalent of bringing statehood through the kitchen door, an old Puerto Rican political adage, but applied to independence in the past.

There seems to be absolutely no interest by the federal government to turn Puerto Rico into a state. On the other hand, there is clearly an interest in up-righting its finances so that bondholders, particularly those that speculated by buying what were fast becoming junk bonds, can get their share of the spoils of the colony.

Because of the excruciatingly slow process for decision-making in the nation (a Democratic President at war with a Republican Congress atop the deliberative nature of Congress itself), it is likely that things will get worse before they get any better. This is aided and abetted by a territorial administration that exacerbates the differences between Congress and the Executive on trying to extract from the U.S. government unique concessions that would allow it to maintain its over 100 plus state agencies, including over three dozen public corporations, some of which are the key culprits in the financial failure of Puerto Rico.

There is surreal parallelism in the Caribbean possible: an island whose governments allowed it to slip under the sea, a metaphor in Isabel Allende's novel on Haiti on becoming independent (An Island under the Sea).

Puerto Rico has yet to slip under the sea on the destruction by its own elected representatives; most likely it will not "slip under the sea." Like Haiti and France Puerto Rico was the darling of American possessions. Mismanagement by the metropolitan power of the relationship between the two led to the creation of the republic of Haiti in 1904. Decisions were made tardily and clumsily in Napoleonic France. So dear had Haiti been to France that Napoleon sent his brother-in-law to put down the revolution. Leclerc came with a part of the Grand Armée and a bevy of notables to straighten out the finances of the colony. Yellow fever, the 19th century version of Zika, did not allow for French control to be reinstated. Allende's metaphor is jolting because Haiti effectively ceased to exist for the purposes of the rest of the world. While not slipping under the sea, for it is buoyed by substantial federal financial transfers, to the rest of the world Puerto Rico is fast becoming a non-entity.

Alejo Carpentier in the novel The Kingdom of this World also explored the theme of Haiti and the destruction by its native rulers. They proclaimed themselves emperors and disposed freely of life and estate. His principal character is a remarkably resilient ex-slave, Ti Noel, who hunkered down in Haiti, surviving the Revolution, always with his freedom in mind, and hunkered down when his master took him to Cuba, preserving what little he had. On his escape from Cuba and returns to Haiti, he hunkered down again in order to preserve his freedom in a limited space.

Most Islanders will hunker down like Ti Noel waiting for the bad times to exhaust themselves.

Is hunkering down an adequate strategy?

It has worked for over five hundred years. There is a clear parallelism with that post-WWII expression in American politics of "staying under the radar."

In practically every home, rich or poor, Islanders built a tormentera by burying at a thirty degree angle half of a long tree trunk and sheathing the extruded half with wooden planks placed at an angle. Since storms did not announce themselves, this was the way they protected themselves during the summer and early autumn months—the storm season for several hundred years. They were still in use in the 1950s. During the rest of the year, distance from the capital city of San Juan and an immense distance from Spain allowed for Islanders an equal respite from political storms as long as they were not noticed by the territorial government.

Hunkering down seems to be part of the cultural DNA or what Roger Bartra calls the exocerebrum (Anthropology of the Brain: Consciousness, Culture, and Free Will, inbunden, 2014), a phenomenon in the mind and culture consisting of the network of beliefs, ways of doing things, ways of thinking including approaching power relationships, language, and even cooking and dress. These constitute a symbolic system that protects every human being from the outside. Every Puerto Rican has his personal tormentera.

Hunkering down is part of the Puerto Rican exocerebrum. This is precisely what led the previous administrations into the destruction of the finances of the territory as economic developed began to slow down in the 1960s; they hunkered down and continued their ways of government waiting for the U.S. to change the relationship imposed on them. This way of government—depleting territorial resources when the economy did not provide—was based on the expectancy that the U.S. would provide another way of government. It became more marked in the 1970s: the U.S. strengthened it by coming through with additional and increases in existing federal programs, transfers and gimmicks (Economic Opportunity grants, Elementary and Secondary Education, Food stamps, Medicaid and, of a different nature but very important for the finance industry, Section 936.)

Hunkering down in order not to change its ways worked under the U.S.! The U.S. always provided! But by the second decade of 21st century there was no more to fritter away.

Is Puerto Rico different?

Ab initio, it was different from anything the U.S. ruled in 1900, even from the Philippines. The U.S. consigned some of the differences in its structure of government; in the relationship with the U.S. Puerto Rico had no say, and still has no vote in Congress (nor does it vote for the President). Puerto Rico was made politically and constitutionally different by the U.S. from anything the U.S. had before the Spanish American war except for the Guano Islands in the Pacific and the Caribbean. The U.S. has tried to maintain said difference.

Puerto Ricans, in their efforts to have political storms pass over them has played the game by making difference a status. They changed the name in the Constitution and endowed it with everything that the U.S. would allow (some parts of the Constitution were disallowed by Congress). In so doing, they pleased the master.

Differential rule applied and allowed in Puerto Rico is a key to its failing condition as a state.

Unlike other major jurisdictions in the United States with failing finances, Puerto Rico is not part of the covey protected by equal application of the law. Unlike with other major jurisdiction, the U.S. can dispose of Puerto Rico at will; the nature of the relationship is chattel, a point repeatedly made by the executive branch since the two White House reports (G.W. Bush and Obama) and by the Attorney General in Hearings in 2015 and 2016 in Congress. During the past forty years efforts to have the U.S. Supreme Court decide on this condition, albeit indirectly, have failed (colonialism, like Medusa's head, turned into stone anyone that looked at it directly); but it agreed to look into the issue during its 2016 spring term when money of American taxpayers was threatened by a local Bankruptcy Law and also on an issue of sovereignty (double exposure in court—the argument being that if Puerto Rico does not have sovereignty or the semblance of sovereignty, cases tried in state court cannot be retried in federal courts).

Puerto Rico is not protected, either, by the national political system of giving and taking for it has no votes in the House or the Senate or the Electoral College. While like Washington D.C. it is sui generis; the similarity stops there. They are both unique and uniquely different in the nation. Washington, D.C. houses the nation's government, thus is unlike anything else in the U.S. The image, the politics, and the mere fact that the rulers on the nation meet in Washington D.C. makes it different from anything else in the U.S.

The only protection of Islanders from its rulers for 500 years has been hunkering down and waiting for something to generate relief. Under Spain it was the situado, the ship laden with silver that stopped in Puerto Rico from Mexico and through the Isthmus of Panamá from Perú, and left some of its silver to run the Island government. This is now the federal transfers, their increase eagerly awaited so that Islanders can continue doing their thing the same way they have had for five hundred years, but subsidized more significantly by the U.S.

What is a failing state?

State failure is the inability or incapacity of a government to provide the services that it determines are absolutely necessary to its population. Thus, if a government tries to provide services that it deems necessary for its population and cannot pay for them or does not have the structure to deliver them, it can drive itself into failure. It is said it is overstretched and that it does not have the income to do provide what it promised. The issue is not that government is too big (this is an ideological presumption; the reality is that the income that the territory can provide its government through taxes and fees is insufficient. This is the case of Puerto Rico.

Particularly damning is the unwillingness or inability of the territorial government to collect taxes. The estimate is of 60% collection of consumer taxes which have piled on each other as each tax fails to meet the required income projections. Rather than go against tax scoffers, a new tax is implemented. The gray economy is estimated at somewhere around 35%. In fact, consumer taxes were instituted to tax consumption of those that did not pay income taxes due by them. This is the acceptance by government of its incapacity or unwillingness to govern, a characteristic of a failing state.

Quiñones and Seda (Argeo T Quiñones-Pérez and Ian J. Seda-Irizarry, "Wealth Extraction, Governmental Servitude, and Social Disintegration in Colonial Puerto Rico," New Politics, Winter 2016) point out this problem directly.

Furthermore, every instance of tax reform from the mid-1980s until 2010 involved lowering taxes in order to promote economic growth—a failed supply side strategy for growth but a very effective tool for income and wealth redistribution to the top. Intensive and indiscriminate use of tax exemptions has made of Puerto Rico a free-for-all fiscal paradise, eroding the tax ethic and tax base of the system. A growing sense of unfairness permeates public opinion. Some events that highlight Puerto Rico's lack of fiscal control are:

- More than 20,000 businesses did not submit income tax reports in April 2014, which meant a loss of revenue on the order of $400 million.
- Big businesses in manufacturing, retail, and other sectors report minimal profits, losses, or breaking even, hiding their revenues through "profit-stripping" strategies with transfer pricing and income shifting.
- Real estate investment trusts siphon hundreds of millions of dollars out of Puerto Rico without paying taxes or being authorized to do business on the island.
- Government bailout payments for debt service of luxury hotels amounted to $400 million during 2012 and 2013.
- Four billion dollars in tax debts went uncollected in 2015. The overall rate of evasion is close to 30% of potential revenues.
- Eighty tax exemption laws together cost over $1 billion in lost revenues yearly.
- Dwindling resources at the Treasury Department for tax enforcement has led to the loss of personnel, intellectual expertise, and technological know-how.
- Tax subsidies at the municipal level, granted by central government, result in $850 million per year in revenue losses for cash-strapped towns.
- Waste of public funds amounts to 10% of the budget according to past comptrollers (equivalent to $900 million of the general fund-backed budget and $2.9 billion of the consolidated budget). Corruption has mounted to almost $900 million of public funds per year, according to FBI figures.

Governor Alejandro García Padilla, on declaring unpayable the public corporation and Commonwealth debt on July 31, 2015, defined Puerto Rico as a failing state and then hunkered down to let the storm pass over him. Jon Purdue (http://www.investors.com/politics/perspective/is-puerto-rico-bankrupt-or-just-unwilling-to-reform/) counters the position of the Governor and summarizes the issues challenging the Governor's position:

Two of the biggest questions surrounding the debate about Puerto Rico's fiscal and economic crises are whether there should be a fiscal control board to oversee a restructuring of the commonwealth's finances, as was done previously with New York and Washington, D.C., and whether Puerto Rico should be granted access to Chapter 9 bankruptcy in order to reorganize portions of its debt.

But perhaps the biggest unresolved question in this debate is whether Puerto Rico is actually insolvent or not. It has so far been unable to produce audited financials for fiscal 2014, despite numerous requests from Congress, while it has been warning of an impending "humanitarian crisis" if it is rebuffed.

But this apocalyptic language was absent when the commonwealth was touting the bonds to investors from which it now wants relief. Thomas Moers Mayer, a representative of two of the largest groups of Puerto Rico bondholders, recently recalled at a forum at the American Enterprise Institute that, "only two years ago the Government Development Bank of Puerto Rico told investors that Puerto Rico could easily repay its debts, that it had one of the lowest ratios of debt per American citizen, because unlike other American citizens, Puerto Ricans are not responsible for the debt of the United States Treasury in that they don't pay federal income taxes."

The Government Development Bank and members of the Puerto Rican government have been telling a different story as of late. Their 2015 "Puerto Rico Fiscal and Economic Growth Plan," put out numbers that claimed that the commonwealth's debt service represents 40% of the general operating budget. That number was disputed in recent congressional testimony by Carlos Colon De Armas, a professor of finance at the University of Puerto Rico, who put the number closer to

16%, when the consolidated budget numbers and alternate revenues are added in. A 40% debt-service load could almost certainly be grounds for claiming insolvency, whereas debt loads of 20% or less have historically been repaid with relatively painless budget restraint. As Colon De Armas puts it, "Utilizing bankruptcy when the debt service burden is 16% is equivalent to saying that 'we can pay our debts, but we'd rather not pay them.'"

Clearly there is a crisis, not humanitarian but of credibility. Purdue follows the analysis of Colón de Armas who suggests that the entire issue is a cover-up for avoiding a serious restructuring of government. Herein is a list of some activities of the territorial Governor.

- He has tried to negotiate some of the debt outside the 1984 Bankruptcy Law (for which Puerto Rico, like other territories, is not eligible).
- He has clawed back on separation of funds to tend to what is essentially preferred debt (Constitutionally guaranteed) reneging on payment of other types of public debt.
- He is accelerating the failure of the public retirement systems by not matching each employee's payment and thus violating the law.
- He has failed to reduce payroll expenses and has publicly said he will not reduce payroll to pay debt. He is driving government service providers into bankruptcy by withholding payments to contractors but also to small businesses and professionals, including payments for services to special children in public schools.
- As of March 2016 he had failed to provide the audited statements of government finances so no one really knows the condition of Puerto Rico's finances except what he shares with the press.

These efforts, whether part of a grander strategy to allow continued hunkering down and maintaining the current government structure or coping with a desperate situation (or both) are moot. The final determination on what a territorial government can or cannot do lies in the federal government. This has been the executive policy and generally the Congressional thrust since the 1990s.

When necessary the Governors will appeal to important world opinion for a with absolutely no hold on the U.S. For example, in February 2016 Governor García Padilla noted that he will appeal to the United Nations (that has absolutely no power or jurisdiction over the U.S.) if the decision by the Supreme Court on double jeopardy in the Sanchez Valle case it will hear in March determines that Puerto Rico lacks even a limited sovereignty for very specific instances of the law.

Another aspect of the relationship with the U.S. brought out by this case is the excruciatingly slow process to even clear up a technical though important aspect of the relationship. When the sovereign does not answer immediately, there is a likelihood of paralysis which is the case of the way the Senate and House have looked into the financial disaster of Puerto Rico. Of course, this is the deliberative nature of the legal system (and also of the legislature). This is the argument of Posner and Vermeule in their thesis of the administrative state that Congress' ways have allowed to administrative state to take over many of its decision-making powers (Eric Posner and Adrian Vermeule, The Executive Unbound: After the Madisonian Republic, Oxford, 2011). Puerto Rico has not been singled out by Congress; it is a victim of a structure that no one controls.

If the territorial government is ineffective in discharging its duties, would Civil Society not impress itself on the leadership to change its ways?

No. There is too much money at stake, even if the Island goes bankrupt.

Civil society, which is the watchdog of government ethics, ceased to discharge this role, and served itself rather than society at large: the assets of government have been filtered into the hands of those that should be its guarantors. Banks, bondholders, unions, NGOs are phagocytic in Puerto Rico. But then this was the pattern carefully taught by the U.S. to Puerto Ricans: allowing corporate America to exploited islanders much as it exploited Latin America for most of the 20th century; President Taft's Dollar Diplomacy seems to be the unaltered policy in the relationship with Puerto Rico.

Civil society is as much at fault as the politicians on whom it calls to protect their assets. Political parties are part of the problem. They are run by elements at times directly in cahoots with unions (which duly re-elect them) and with bonding houses and banks that finance them.

In Puerto Rico, the electoral system ceased to be a mechanism for change in a failed state because political parties, which are an important part of civil society, merely recycle those that are dipping their hands in the till for their favorite factions, defending the few for the many even while mouthing populist slogans.

Civil society absconded with the government til in Puerto Rico. The problem is not only mismanagement by the territorial government but rampant corruption. (See one the last point made by Quiñones and Seda). This includes for profit corporations posing as NGOs; for profit corporations, banking and financial institutions that have become rentists like Section 936 corporations in the past and foreign corporations (Controlled Foreign Corporations) with substantial federal tax abatement; land and assets speculators that have been given local tax abatement in exchange for living in Puerto Rico; government unions that can sway elections through their organizing power thus assuring a drain in resources of public corporations. Churches are part of the institutional network that lives and thrives in clientelism thus it is not in their interest to recognize moral and ethical dilemmas.

Why is there no mention of the fragility of the state in Puerto Rico?

America does not fail. Commonwealth is a creation of Congress, with the support of the Presidency and the Supreme Court. American endeavors are not supposed to fail, and when they fail, they are buried under tons of dollars. Puerto Ricans are cognizant of Congress' penchant to throw money at problems so they are demanding a ton of dollars that on burying Commonwealth will, paradoxically, save it. Civil society is particularly avid of mana from Washington, D.C. The continued failure of Puerto Rico is in the interest of many since it will be propped up by Congress just as it was by Section 936.

- It is under the political radar of the nation except in exceptional circumstances (the Vieques fracas) when major factions of the nation could be affected (in Vieques, it the rejection of militarism as represented by the U.S. Navy). Were Puerto Rico able to pay what it owes, it would be under the radar and, effectively, it is under the radar for the purposes of factions other than financial that spurred Congress into action. Also, Puerto Rico is effectively propped by federal transfers.

- On the other hand, recognition of failure might lead the federal government to change the relationship that led to this disaster. There are too many other interests buttressing the current relationship; it is good business to significant groups in the nation. Given the political implications of this financial problem (not unlike Vieques) it is possible that the current administration claim that had Puerto Rico had the powers that the Popular Democratic Party (from 1953 through 1968 and from 1984 thought 1992) and the people of Puerto Rico requested in the 1967 plebiscite (60.1%), it would possible have been able to avert failure. Speculative? Yes. But a possible perception.

- Is the nation endangered by the crisis in Puerto Rico? Clearly not, but it has been systematically threatened by the national administration and the local administration with a humanitarian crisis. (Effectively this was the argument sustaining the issue of Vieques, a humanitarian crisis in the lives of some 12,000 persons).

- While it is also speculative that the territorial administration is trying to generate a humanitarian crisis, it is clearly trying to generate conditions not dissimilar to Vieques that attracted national attention. The Governor's statement that Puerto Rico cannot pay back its debt must be supported by certified audit of government income and expenditures and operations. The 2013–2014 statement has yet to be issue in February 2016.

- Locally, the territorial government shields the territorial civil society and its government employment payroll in refusing to share information on its finances. It speaks of decreases in debt (from $71 billion to $69) but is driving the retirement systems into faster bankruptcy by withholding matching payments made by retirees and has over $1.8 billion in unpaid debts to suppliers.

- The economic disaster brewing since the oil shock of 1973 was not critical to the nation; it came slowly and quietly, (Carl Sandberg would have said "on little cat's 'feet'." Federal transfer payments masked the problem which is quite different from that of the financial crisis. An economically disastrous decade (2006–1015) confirming Puerto Rico's development failure did not generate a crisis in the nation. It has no votes in Congress and has zero presidential electors.

- The Obama administration emphasis on Cuba will soon have its political effects on Puerto Rico. How can so much attention be paid to a foreign country and so little to a territory of the nation peopled by U.S. citizens?

Who is responsible for this mess?

This is the question to ask when someone seeks a whipping boy.

The problem is structural and has been building up for a long time. By nature, Congress is deliberative, not given the action or execution of programs. The problem is not that it has failed its ministerial duty but that it is not in its design to act as an executive. The last two administrations provided some guidance but no action with two White House Presidential reports on the condition of Puerto Rico, insisting that it is for Congress to act. Furthermore the Administrative State, the real Fourth power of the nation, is quite content with fiddling with the problem and recommending piecemeal actions when a concerted approach is necessary.

The issue is not who is right or not (Congress, the Executive or the Administrative State) or who brought about this disaster (Islanders or the federal government). The problem is how are we to prevent it from happening again once it is up righted. Islanders have provided only tentative answers and suggestions, which is understandable. It is an election year and administrations have changed in the last four elections.

In a representative government only those that vote matter, except in a crisis that turns into a political embarrassment: the indifference shown to the problems besetting Commonwealth since mid-century as a result of the Truman Doctrine of disengagement from Puerto Rico and particularly since 2006, and the attention paid to one or another corporate group, defense interest, or financial institutions requires serious attention. These paragraphs do not fulfill such a requirement but should work as an enticement in that direction.

From 1970 to 2015 Puerto Rico went from the darling in U.S. foreign policy to accursed.

What has happened? Puerto Rico is no longer important for foreign policy, defense, and commerce; only to a small group of bond holders. Will it continue to be disposable once the bond holders are insulated from greater damage?

The federal government has repeatedly said there are no other changes possible than independence or statehood; the two White House reports on Puerto Rico 2009 (Bush) and 2011 (Obama) confirmed it. A continuation of the current relationship, now proven toxic, might be possible with some temporary concessions by Congress.

Special Concessions do not make for economic development

What happened the last time the some concessions were made? When Congress finds better things to do with those concessions, it will take them away. Puerto Rico is powerless to defend itself from Congress. But then, this is the nature of republican government. This is why the Senate hearings were critical to Puerto Rico.

The grand concession in mid-century was unique access to the U.S. market and tax abatement. Subsequently, the U.S. market was opened to most of the Third World and, the same time, labor and other environmental demands by the federal government made its light manufacturing less competitive. When the condition of Puerto Rico was recognized as dire in 1973 as a result of the oil crisis, tax abatement was enhanced (Section 936, 1976). Twenty years later Section 936 was struck by Congress. If past Congressional action is an indication of future action, Puerto Rico can expect something to mask its condition but not solve it. There are too many interests propping up Commonwealth. A Financial Board is a possibility, but can it preserve (or recognize) some autonomy for the territorial government? Would it have the power to withhold money from agencies, thus eliminating some of them? Is this a goal? Would it have the power to determine an order of payment of debts (bonds vs retirement, the currently retired vs those to retire in the future?) Will it allow for some kind or limited debt restructuring outside of the Bankruptcy Act of 1984?

Possibly the most important question is how would its action could lead into strengthening the economy rather than just solve the immediate conundrum of debt payment? Most economists agree that the economic problems are based on the relationship with the U.S. What Congress gives, Congress can take away without any consideration as to the welfare or well-being of Puerto Rico and Puerto Rican islanders. When Congress legislates, it can leave Puerto Rico out as in the 1984 Bankruptcy Act, include it as a special consideration for some faction in Congress as in section 936, or make it part of a law applicable to the entire nation as environmental protection laws and minimum wage and other aspects of labor protection.

In answering these questions, Congress might consider that the fight for the political parties (outside of the corruption that feeds them on winning an election) is centered on imposing one or another status solution. Profligate spending was tied with the generation of jobs that, in turn, generated votes. The context was a tanking economy.

Congress has been provided with two different points of view by businessmen and economists.

1. The financial crisis is the product of profligacy and a tanking economy, so it must be solved through bankruptcy proceedings and additional funds from Congress plus concessions such as elimination of minimum wage and of cabotage laws. It essentially leaves out restructuring and downsizing of government as a principal activity.

2. The financial crisis is the product of profligacy but not of the tanking economy, so it must be solved through belt tightening, restructuring government, and reorganization and direction of the income of the territory in activities with a clear return on investment (including examining all tax abatement measures).

The second point seems to have the attention of most Republicans in Congress since ideologically all territories must pay their way. It would be shortsighted, although still an immense relief, if Congress were to adopt the second point of view without looking into the need of changing the relationship of Puerto Rico and the United States now recognized as toxic for economic development. There should be minimally two agendas: an action agenda on the debt (including all government debt and retirement program shortfalls), and a study and deliberative agenda on the relationship of Puerto Rico and the U.S. with recommendations for actions. In both agendas having such actions triggered by companion actions by the territorial government. If you do this, we will do this. thus the final decision is of the territorial government.

○